The
End-Times

by the Ancient Church Fathers

By Ken Johnson, Th.D.

Copyright 2016, by Ken Johnson, Th.D.

The End-Times by the Ancient Church Fathers
by Ken Johnson, Th.D.

Printed in the United States of America

ISBN – 10: 1532791402
ISBN – 13: 978-1532791406

Unless otherwise indicated, Bible quotations from the church fathers are their own paraphrase of their Greek or Latin text.

Contents

Introduction 8
    The Six Thousand Years 13
    The First Century AD 16
    Justin Martyr 17
    Irenaeus' End-Time Teaching 18
        Premillennialism 18
        Pre-Trib Rapture 18
        The Time of the End Begins 18
        Roman Empire 18
        The Ten Nations 19
        Abomination of Desolation 19
        Antichrist from the Tribe of Dan 19
        The Number 666 20
        Summary of Irenaeus' End-Time teaching 20
    Ephrem's *The End Times* 23
        1a Introduction 23
        1b Rome Divided, Then Dissolved 23
        2a Turn Toward Holiness 24
        2b Pre-Tribulation Rapture 25
        3 In The Desert, People Become Senseless 26
        4 The Worthless Nations Arise 26
        5a Origin of the Ten Nations 27
        5b Antichrist from the Tribe of Dan 28
        6 Origin of the Antichrist 28
        7 The First 3.5 Years – Ps. 83 29
        8 The Second 3.5 Years 30

9 Enoch and Elijah 31
10 The Second Coming 32
Summary of *The End Times* 33

Hippolytus' *The Antichrist* 36
1-4 General Introduction 36
5 Prophecy Introduction 40
6 Symbols of the Christ and Antichrist 41
7 Messiah from Judah 42
8 Messiah Resurrects After Three Days 42
9 Messiah a Descendant of David 44
10 The Jews and Gentiles in One Faith 44
11 Messiah's atoning Death 44
12 Messiah Testified by the Prophets 45
13 Messiah's Commands Are Pure 45
14 Antichrist from the Tribe of Dan 45
15 No Jewish King Came from the Tribe of Dan ... 46
16 Antichrist called the Assyrian – Isaiah 10 47
17 Antichrist – Isaiah 14 48
18 Antichrist – Ezekiel 28 50
19 Nebuchadnezzar's Image 51
20 Daniel's Beast Vision 51
21 The Judgment of the Beast 52
22 Daniel's Vision of Messiah 53
23 Daniel's Winged Lion – Babylon 53
24a Daniel's Bear – Medo-Persia 54
24b Daniel's Leopard – Greece 54
25a Daniel's Non-Descript Beast – Rome 54
25b Ten Toes / Horns 55
25c Three Kingdoms Against the Antichrist 55
26 The Stone – Messianic Kingdom 56
27 Future Ten Kingdoms 57

28 Summary of the Image and Daniel's Beasts 57
29 We Should Reveal the Mysteries 57
30 Jerusalem Literally Destroyed 58
31 Many Spoke of Her 59
32 The Accuracy of Daniel 59
33 Rome Still Rules – 60
34-35 The Harlot – Isaiah 60
36-42 The Harlot – Revelation 62
43 Summary of the Harlot 68
44a The Two Advents of Messiah 68
44b-46a The Witness of the First Coming 69
46b Second Coming Witnesses 71
47 The Timing of the Two Witnesses 71
48 The Earth Beast 73
49 Earth Beast Explained 74
50 The Number of the Beast 76
51 Jordan Falls to the Antichrist 77
52 Tyre and Beirut Fall to the Antichrist 77
53 Pride of the Antichrist 78
54 Antichrist Gathers His Army 79
55 The Partridge Allegory 80
56 Antichrist's Army Persecutes the Saints 80
57a Luke's Parable Explained 81
57b Micah's Assyrian Antichrist 82
58a Antichrist Uses the Jews 82
58b-59 Antichrist's Ethiopia 83
60-61 The Sun-clad Woman 84
62-63 The Abomination of Desolation 87
64a The Two Halves of the Tribulation 89
64b Pre-Trib Rapture 90
65 The Resurrection 91

66-67 Rapture 93
Summary of *The Antichrist* 94

Hippolytus' *On the End of the World* 97
1-2 General Introduction 97
3 The Church Shall Apostatize 98
4 Antichrist's Scorching Eastern Wind 99
5-6 The Church is left Desolate 100
7 End-Time Church Described 102
8 The Signs 103
9 False Christs 104
10-11 Heresies in the Church 105
12 Nebuchadnezzar's Great Image 107
13 Daniel's Vision of Beasts 108
14 Daniel's Lioness 109
15 Daniel's Bear and Leopard 109
16-17 Daniel's Roman Beast 110
18a The Tribe of Judah 111
18b-19 The Tribe of Dan 112
20 Symbols of Christ and the Antichrist 114
21 Enoch, Elijah, and John 114
22 Antichrist's Supposed Virgin Birth 116
23-25a Antichrist's Deception 117
25b The Antichrist Wars 119
26a The Demonic Host 120
26b False Signs 121
27 The Judgment 122
28 The Mark 122
29-30 Antichrist and the Two Witnesses 124
31 The Minions of the Beast 125
32 The Believers 126
33-34 The Famines 126

 35 Time Shortened 128
 36 Second Coming of the Messiah 128
 37 Rapture or White Throne Judgment? 130
 38-40 Judgment of the Wicked 130
 41 Sheep and Goat Judgement 133
 Summary of *On The End of the World* 134

Conclusion 138

Index of Bible References 143

Other Books and DVDs by Ken Johnson, Th.D. 146

Bibliography 158

Introduction

In this work we want to focus on the disciples of the apostles and what they taught about the end times. The church fathers are not authoritative in the same sense as the Holy Scriptures; but if they all teach the same doctrine and state they were taught these things from the apostles, then I think it is a safe bet that this apostolic teaching is correct. We should note that even if they were correct, the writings could be garbled or mistranslated in places. If we compare them with Scripture and history, we should be able to get a much closer look into the end times than we ever have before.

In the chart on the next page you can see that Polycarp and Ignatius were students of the apostle John. Polycarp worked with John in ministry before and after John wrote the book of Revelation on the Isle of Patmos in AD 95. John died and was buried in the city of Ephesus while Polycarp continued the work of planting churches in the area until his own death by martyrdom.

Irenaeus
Irenaeus was born in in Smyrna in AD 130. He became a student of Polycarp and testified that he occasionally spoke to the very old apostle John. In approximately AD 170, Irenaeus wrote a five-volume work entitled *Against Heresies*. It deals mostly with the cults and heretics of his

Introduction

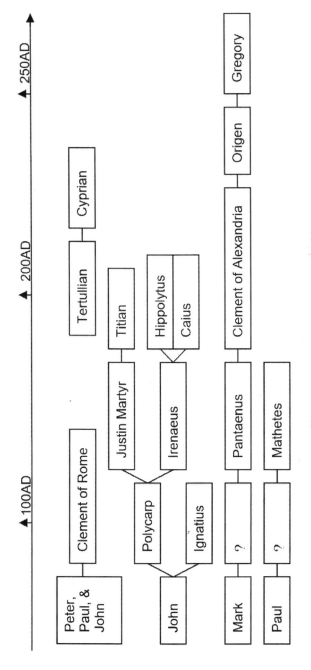

The End Times by the Ancient Church Fathers

day but also touches on prophecy, especially when there was a cult that was misinterpreting a biblical prediction for its own purposes. Our first section on prophecy deals with how Irenaeus taught end-time prophecy. Irenaeus died in Lugdunum, France, in AD 202.

Justin Martyr
Justin was born in Nablus, Israel, in AD 100. As a student of Polycarp, he wrote several works on various topics, including Bible prophecy. He taught the same doctrines about prophecy that Irenaeus did. He was eventually martyred in Rome in AD 165 for being a Christian.

Hippolytus
Church father Hippolytus was a student of Irenaeus. He was born in AD 170. Hippolytus wrote *Against All Heresies* against the cults of his time. He stood against two of the Roman Catholic popes of his day because they were teaching heresy for money and were involved in gross immorality. For his testimony and historical information, see *Gnostic Origins of Roman Catholicism*. Eventually Pope Callixtus I was removed from office. Hippolytus would have been the next Pope of Rome but Callixtus refused to step down. His refusal created two popes. When this happened, the erring pope was still referred to as pope, but the replacement who was not powerful enough to expel the old pope was called an antipope. What this means for us is that a very high-ranking Roman Catholic saint (almost a full pope himself) taught protestant theology. We see this when looking at the two works authored by Hippolytus dealing

Introduction

specifically with end-time prophecy. The first one is entitled *The Antichrist*. The second one is entitled *The End Times*. Hippolytus died AD 235

Ephrem the Syrian
In AD 306, in the Eastern Church, a man called Ephrem the Syrian was born. He, too, testified that he studied under those who knew Christians who had studied under the apostles. Ephrem authored numerous books, commentaries, and lecture series. One such work was entitled *The End Times*. Today it is referred to by many as Pseudo-Ephrem. Many who do not believe in a pre-trib rapture think this work is called Pseudo-Ephrem because it is a fake document. In fact, the reason it is called Pseudo-Ephrem is because two church fathers quote the work and state it was authored by Ephrem the Syrian, while one other church father stated he believed it was authored by Isadore of Seville. No church father questions the work's validity, just the identity of the author. So, with the testimony of two church fathers, it is called Pseudo-Ephrem and not Pseudo-Isadore. Ephrem died June 9, AD 373 in Edessa, Turkey.

Other church fathers wrote about end time prophecy including: Tertullian, Cyprian, Commodianus, Victorinus, Methodius, Origen, Lactantius, and Nepos.

The Scope of this Work
For our purposes, we wanted to put together the actual commentaries from the most ancient church fathers on the subject of end-time prophecy. We have the basic outline

The End Times by the Ancient Church Fathers

of prophecy with a few interesting notes from Irenaeus' *Against Heresies*. We have also produced, in their entirety, the one commentary from Ephrem and two from Hippolytus.

What we will find is that anciently, the highest scholars of the Roman Catholic and Eastern Orthodox institutions agree with the first-century disciples of the apostles whose doctrine agrees with modern Protestant interpretation of Bible prophecy. We will not only verify the basics in Bible prophecy, but will learn some startling details from them as well.

The Six Thousand Years

The idea that Jesus will return to set up His millennial kingdom in the Jewish year 6,000 is taught by several ancient church fathers. The first coming of Jesus Christ was about 4,000 years after Creation. These ancient church fathers taught the Second Coming would be about AD 2000. The most descriptive is in the Epistle of Barnabas which devotes an entire chapter on this issue. Remember, this does not mean they were correct; but if they believed and taught this, it proves the ancient Christians were premillennial. Here are a few quotes on the issue. With the calendars being confused and inaccurate, we can't say for certain when the year 6,000 will occur. An approximate range would be between the years AD 2030 and 2067, although it could occur even earlier. See *Ancient Post-Flood History* for more information on the historical timeline.

Barnabas, AD First Century
"Therefore, children, in six days, or in six thousand years, all the prophecies will be fulfilled. Then it says, 'He rested on the seventh day.' This signifies at the Second Coming of our Lord Jesus, He will destroy the Antichrist, judge the ungodly, and change the sun, moon, and stars. Then He will truly rest during the Millennial reign, which is the seventh day." *Epistle of Barnabas 15:7-9*

The End Times by the Ancient Church Fathers

Irenaeus, AD 180
"The day of the Lord is as a thousand years; and in six days created things were completed. It is evident, therefore, they will come to an end in the six thousandth year." *Against Heresies 5.28*

Hippolytus, AD 205
"The Sabbath is a type of the future kingdom... For "a day with the Lord is as a thousand years." Since, then, in six days the Lord created all things, it follows that in six thousand years all will be fulfilled." *Fragment 2; Commentary on Daniel 2.4*

Commodianus, AD 240
"We will be immortal when the six thousand years are completed." *Against the Gods of the Heathens 35*
"Resurrection of the body will be when six thousand years are completed, and after the one thousand years [millennial reign], the world will come to an end." *Against the Gods of the Heathens 80*

Victorinus, AD 240
"Satan will be bound until the thousand years are finished; that is, after the sixth day."
Commentary on Revelation 20.1-3

Methodius, AD 290
"In the seventh millennium we will be immortal and truly celebrate the Feast of Tabernacles." *Ten Virgins 9.1*

The Six Thousand Years

Lactantius, AD 304
"The sixth thousandth year is not yet complete. When this number is complete, the consummation must take place."
Divine Institutes 7.14

The First Century AD

In this small section I wanted to show that some early Christians wrote about prophecy, and that they all taught the same things. In the first century only Barnabas and Papias (to my knowledge) wrote about Bible prophecy.

> "I was taught by the Apostle John, himself, that after the resurrection of the dead, Jesus will personally reign for one thousand years."
> *Papias, Fragment 6*

> "You can perceive that their hope is vain. Furthermore, the Lord said, 'Behold, they who destroy this temple, even they will again build it up once more.' This prophecy was fulfilled because the Jews went to war against their enemy. But even though they are now no more than servants to Rome, they will return and rebuild the temple. It was revealed that the city of Jerusalem, the temple, and the people of Israel were to be given up." *Epistle of Barnabas 16:5-7*

Papias was blessed to have been taught Bible prophecy by John the Apostle. Barnabas was the first to tell us that the Jews would return to their land and rebuild their Jerusalem temple.

First Century

Justin Martyr

"The Man of Sin, spoken of by Daniel, will rule two [three] times and a half, before the Second Advent." *Justin Martyr, Dialogue 32*

"There will be a literal one-thousand-year reign of Christ." *Justin Martyr, Dialogue 81*

"The man of apostasy, who speaks strange things against the Most High, shall venture to do unlawful deeds on the earth against believers." *Justin Martyr, Dialogue 110*

We can see that Justin taught that the future Antichrist will have his complete dominion in the second half of the tribulation period, or the last three-and-a-half years. Notice some copies of the text say "two and a half." I wanted to make you aware that sometimes there are scribal errors that creep into a text. Justin also taught the Antichrist will persecute believers and will be destroyed by Jesus Christ upon His Second Coming.

Irenaeus' End-Time Teaching

Premillennialism
"There is a resurrection of the Just that takes place after the destruction of the Antichrist and all nations under his rule. Many believers will make it through the Tribulation and replenish the earth. In the Resurrection we will have fellowship and communion with the holy angels, and union with spiritual beings. The new heavens and earth are first created and then the new Jerusalem descends. These are all literal things, and Christians who allegorize them are immature Christians." *Against Heresies 5.35*

Pre-Trib Rapture
"When in the end that church will suddenly be caught up from this, then it is said, 'There will be tribulation such as not been since the beginning, nor will be.'"
Against Heresies 5.29

The Time of the End Begins
"Daniel the prophet says 'Shut up the words, and seal the book even to the time of consummation, until many learn, and knowledge be completed.' For at that time, when the dispersion shall be accomplished [1948], they shall know all these things." *Against Heresies 4.26*

Roman Empire
"The Roman Empire will first be divided and then be dissolved." *Against Heresies 5.26*

"The fourth kingdom seen by Daniel is Rome. The rebuilt temple will be in Jerusalem." *Against Heresies 5.30*

The Ten Nations
Ten kings will arise from what used to be the Roman Empire. The Antichrist slays three of the kings and he is then the eighth king among them. The kings will destroy Babylon, then give the Babylonian kingdom to the Beast and put the believers to flight. After that, they will be destroyed by the coming of the Lord. Daniel's horns are the same as the ten toes. The toes being part iron and part clay mean some kings will be active and strong while others, weak and inactive. And the kings will not agree with each other." *Against Heresies 5.26*

Abomination of Desolation
"In 2 Thessalonians, the 'falling away' is an apostasy and there will be a literal rebuilt temple. In Matthew [chapter 24], the 'abomination spoken by Daniel' is the Antichrist sitting in the temple as if he were Christ. The abomination will start in the middle of Daniel's 70th week and last for a literal three years and six months. The little horn [11th] is the Antichrist." *Against Heresies 5.25*

Antichrist from the Tribe of Dan
"The Antichrist shall come from the tribe of Dan. That is why the tribe of Dan is not mentioned in the Apocalypse." *Against Heresies 5.30*

The End Times by the Ancient Church Fathers

The Number 666

"The name of the Antichrist equals 666 if spelled out in Greek. Do not even try to find out the number of the name until the ten kings arise. Titan is one Greek word that totals 666. [Each letter in Greek also represents a number, so every Greek word also totals a number.]"
Against Heresies 5.30

Summary of Irenaeus' End-Time teaching

All mature Christians are premillennial; they believe in a future seven-year tribulation with the appearance of the Antichrist. They also believe in a literal one-thousand-year reign of Jesus Christ which starts at His Second Coming when Jesus defeats the Antichrist. Irenaeus may or may not have the correct order when he says there will be a physical resurrection, then Millennial Reign, then new heavens and new earth, and the New Jerusalem, but he knows they are literal events.

He accurately understood from Scripture that the Roman Empire would divide into two separate empires before it would be dissolved. Irenaeus wrote these predictions about AD 170. The Roman Empire became Christian in AD 325, divided into two parts (Rome and Constantinople) in AD 395, and dissolved in AD 476.

The End Times - Irenaeus

Irenaeus taught the image dream of Nebuchadnezzar and the beast dreams of Daniel predicted the same empires ruling over Israel. The first was the Babylonian Empire, represented by the head of gold and the winged lion. The second was the Medio-Persian Empire, represented by the chest and arms of silver, the bear, and the ram. The third was the Grecian Empire represented by the thighs of brass, the leopard, and the goat. The fourth was the Roman Empire represented by legs of iron and the nondescript beast. Out of the Roman Empire will come the ten nations, symbolized by the horns and toes. The eleventh horn will be the Antichrist himself, who will destroy three of the ten nations and become the leader of the remaining seven.

The end times begin when Israel returns as a nation, which sparks a series of prophecies to be fulfilled, helping us to correctly interpret the rest of the prophecies. The church in general will become apostate. Then the true church will be raptured before the Tribulation begins. The Antichrist will enforce a covenant for seven years, at the end of which is the Second Coming of Jesus Christ to earth and the start of the Millennial Reign.

In addition to this basic outline of prophecy, Irenaeus added some very helpful details. One is that the Antichrist's name equals 666 when it is spelled out in Greek. Another is that the Antichrist will be born from the tribe of Dan. We will see details to these and other mysteries from Ephrem and Hippolytus.

The End Times by the Ancient Church Fathers

Irenaeus' End-Time Outline

1. The Church apostatizes
2. Antichrist born in Dan

Start of Seven Years
3. Rapture of the Church
4. Rebuilding of a Jerusalem temple
5. The ten nations destroy Mystery Babylon

Middle of Seven Years
6. The Antichrist sets up a desolating abomination
7. The ten nations persecute believers

End of Seven Years
8. Second Coming
9. Establishment of the Millennium
10. Building of the Millennial Temple

Ephrem's *The End Times*

1a Introduction

Dearly beloved brothers, believe the Holy Spirit who speaks in us. We have already told you that the end of the world is near, the coming "consummation." Faith is withering away among mankind. How many foolish things are seen among the youth, crimes among bishops, lies among pastors, and perjuries among deacons! There are evil deeds among the ministers, adulteries in the aged, wantonness in the youths — in mature women false faces, in virgins dangerous traces! In the midst of all this there are the wars with the Persians, and we see struggles with diverse nations threatening and "kingdom rising against kingdom.[a]"

1b Rome Divided, Then Dissolved

When the Roman Empire begins to be consumed by the sword, the coming of the Evil One is at hand.[b] It is necessary that the world come to an end after the completion of the Roman Empire. In those days two brothers[c] will come to the Roman Empire who will rule with one mind; but because one will surpass the other,

---

[a] Matthew 24:7

[b] He is teaching that after the Roman Empire is dissolved then the ten nations will appear and the Antichrist will be revealed.

[c] Emperor Theodosius' sons Arcadius and Honorius inherited the east and west halves of the Empire respectively. This schism occurred in AD 395. Ephrem may have gotten the idea of two brothers from the *Ezra Apocalypse 11-12*.

there will be a schism between them. And so the Adversary will be loosed and will stir up hatred between the Persian and Roman empires.[d] In those days many will rise up against Rome; the Jewish people will be her adversaries.[e] There will be stirrings of nations and evil reports, pestilences, famines, and earthquakes in various places. All nations will receive captives; there will be wars and rumors of wars. From the rising to the setting of the sun, the sword will devour much. The times will be so dangerous that in fear and trembling they will not permit thoughts of better things, because many will be the oppressions and desolations of regions that are to come.

2a Turn Toward Holiness

Therefore, my brothers, we should thoroughly understand what is imminent or overhanging. Already there have been hunger and plagues, violent movements of nations and signs, which have been predicted by the Lord. These have already been fulfilled, nothing else remains, except the advent of the Wicked One after the completion of the Roman kingdom. Why then are we so focused with worldly business, and our minds so fixed on worldly desires and the anxieties of the ages? Shouldn't we reject every care of earthly actions and prepare ourselves to meet the Lord Christ, so that he may draw us[f] from the

---

[d] The Byzantine-Persian wars (AD 602-628)
[e] The Byzantine Empire fell in AD 1453 to the Muslim Ottoman Empire. Enoch 56 predicts a war between a revived Israel and Iran (Persia). Ephrem could also be predicting a war between Israel and a revived Roman Empire (the ten nations).
[f] Only those looking for the Rapture will be taken up from the coming wrath.

confusion, which overwhelms all the world? Dearest brother, the coming of the Lord is nigh, because the end of the world is at hand, it is the very last time. Or will you not believe unless you see it with your own eyes? Do not let the prophet's saying be fulfilled among you which declares:

> "Woe to those who desire to see the day of the Lord!" *Amos 6:18*

2b Pre-Tribulation Rapture

For all the saints and elect of God are gathered, prior to the tribulation that is to come, and are taken to the Lord[g] lest they see the confusion that will overwhelm the world because of our sins. And so, dear brothers, it is the eleventh hour, and the end of the world comes to the harvest, and angels, armed and prepared, hold sickles in their hands, awaiting the empire of the Lord. And we think that the world is completely blind to this, arriving at its downfall early. Commotions are happening, wars of diverse peoples, battles, incursions of the barbarians threaten, and countries are being desolated. We seem neither afraid when hearing the rumors of wars nor seeing them appear. We should repent! If we are afraid of them it is because we do not wish to be changed; we need to repent of that too!

---

[g] Believers are raptured in a pre-tribulation rapture.

The End Times by the Ancient Church Fathers

3 In The Desert, People Become Senseless

When the end of the world comes, there arise diverse wars, commotions on all sides, horrible earthquakes, perturbations of nations, tempests throughout the lands, plagues, famine, drought, great danger throughout the sea and dry land, constant persecutions, slaughters and massacres everywhere, fear in the homes, panic in the cities, quaking in the thoroughfares, suspicions in the male, anxiety in the streets. In the desert, people become senseless; spirits melt in the cities. A friend will not be grieved over a friend, neither a brother for a brother, nor parents for their children, nor a faithful servant for his master, but one inevitability shall overwhelm them all; neither is anyone able to be recovered in that time[h], who has not been made completely aware of the coming danger, but all people, who have been constricted by fear, are consumed because of the overhanging evils.

4 The Worthless Nations Arise

Whenever, therefore, the earth is agitated by the nations, people will hide themselves from the wars in the mountains and rocks, by caves and caverns of the earth, by graves and memorials of the dead, and there, as they waste away gradually by fear, they draw breath, because there is not any place at all to flee, but there will be concession and intolerable pressure. And those who are in the east will flee to the west, and moreover, those who are in the west shall flee to the east, and there is not a safer place anywhere, because the world shall be overwhelmed

---

[h] Those who have taken the mark of the beast cannot be saved.

The End Times - Ephrem

by worthless nations[i], whose aspect appears to be of wild animals more than that of men. Because those very much horrible nations, most profane and most defiled, who do not spare lives, and shall destroy the living from the dead, shall consume the dead, they eat dead flesh[j], they drink the blood of beasts[k], they pollute the world, contaminate all things, and the one who is able to resist them is not there. In those days people shall not be buried, neither Christian, nor heretic, neither Jew, nor pagan; because of fear and dread, there is not one who buries them; because all people, while they are fleeing, ignore them.

5a Origin of the Ten Nations

Whenever the days of the times of those nations have been fulfilled, after they have destroyed the earth, it shall rest; but first, the Roman kingdom is removed from everyday life, and the empire of the Christians is handed down by God.[l] The end comes when the prophecy of the Roman kingdom begins to be fulfilled; the prophecy of all the dominions and powers.[m]

---

[i] Modern day Islamic nations
[j] We have seen in our day, Syrian rebels (Muslim) cut out the enemy's heart and eat it.
[k] Muslim rebels in Indonesia are famous for the "death oaths" where they kill a dog and drink its blood before they go to war.
[l] First, pagan Rome becomes Christian Rome (AD 325). Then Rome is divided (AD 395). Then the western Roman Empire falls (AD 476). Then the Eastern Roman Empire falls (AD 1453).
[m] Rome is the last of the beastly nations seen by Daniel before the advent of the ten nations.

5b Antichrist from the Tribe of Dan

Then that worthless and abominable dragon shall appear[n], he, whom Moses named in Deuteronomy, saying:

> "Dan[o] is a young lion, reclining and leaping from Bashan." *Deuteronomy 33:22*

Because he reclines in order that he may seize, destroy, and slay. Indeed, he is a young whelp of a lion, not as the lion of the tribe of Judah, but roaring because of his wrath, that he may devour. "And he leaps out from Bashan." "Bashan" certainly is interpreted "confusion." He shall rise up from the confusion of his iniquity. The one who gathers together to himself a "partridge the children of confusion"[p], also shall call them, whom he has not brought forth, just as Jeremiah the prophet says.[q] Also in the last day they shall relinquish him just as confused.

6 Origin of the Antichrist

When therefore the end of the world comes, that abominable, lying, and murderous one is born from the tribe of Dan. He is conceived from the seed of a man and from an unclean or most vile virgin, mixed with an evil or

---

[n] The Antichrist's kingdom will come after the fall of the Roman Empire and after the apostasy of Christian Rome.

[o] The tribe of Dan originally settled on the coast of Israel, but after troubles from the Philistines to the south, they migrated to the area of Bashan (the Golan Heights area). The Antichrist will be born in that region of modern-day Syria.

[p] Or children of Sheth. The Messiah destroys the children of Sheth at the Second Coming. See Numbers 24:17 KJV

[q] Jeremiah 17:11

worthless spirit. But that abominable corrupter, more of spirits than of bodies, while a youth, the crafty dragon appears under the appearance of righteousness, before he takes the kingdom. Because he will be craftily gentle to all people, not receiving gifts, not placed before another person, loving to all people, quiet to everyone, not desiring gifts, appearing friendly among close friends, so that men may bless him, saying "he is a just man," not knowing that a wolf lies concealed under the appearance of a lamb, and that a greedy man is inside under the skin of a sheep.

7 The First 3.5 Years – Ps. 83

Before the time of the abomination of his desolation,[r] having been made legal, he takes the empire, and, just as it is said in the Psalm:

> "They have been made for the undertaking for the sons of Lot." *Psalm 83:8*

the Moabites and the Ammonites shall meet him first as their king. Therefore, when he receives the kingdom, he orders the temple of God to be rebuilt for himself, which is in Jerusalem; who, after coming into it, he shall sit as God and order that he be adored by all nations, since he is carnal, filthy, and mixed with worthless spirit and flesh. Then that eloquence shall be fulfilled of Daniel the prophet:

---

[r] The image placed in the rebuilt Jewish temple. See Daniel 11:31; 12:11 and Revelation 13:15

The End Times by the Ancient Church Fathers

> "And he shall not know the God of their fathers, and he shall not know the desires of women."
> *Daniel 11:37*

Because the very wicked serpent shall direct every worship to himself. Because he shall put forth an edict so that people may be circumcised according to the rite of the old law.[s] Then the Jews shall congratulate him, because he gave them again the practice of the first covenant; then all people from everywhere shall flock together to him at the city of Jerusalem, and the holy city shall be trampled on by the nations for forty-two months, just as the holy apostle says in the Apocalypse, which become three and a half years, 1,260 days.

8 The Second 3.5 Years

In these three years and a half the heaven shall suspend its dew; because there will be no rain upon the earth, and the clouds shall cease to pass through the air, and the stars shall be seen with difficulty in the sky because of the excessive dryness, which happens in the time of the very fierce dragon. Because all great rivers and very powerful fountains that overflow with themselves shall be dried up, torrents shall dry up their water-courses because of the intolerable age, and there will be a great tribulation, as there has not been, since people began to be upon the earth, and there will be famine and an insufferable thirst. And children shall waste away in the bosom of their

---

[s] Ephrem seems to indicate that "not regarding the desire of women" equates to reviving the Jewish rite of mandatory circumcision.

mothers, and wives upon the knees of their husbands, by not having victuals to eat. Because there will be in those days lack of bread and water, and no one is able to sell or to buy of the grain of the fall harvest, unless he is one who has the serpentine sign[t] on the forehead or on the hand. Then gold and silver and precious clothing or precious stones shall lie along the streets, and also even every type of pearls along the thoroughfares and streets of the cities, but there is not one who may extend the hand and take or desire them, but they consider all things as good as nothing because of the extreme lack and famine of bread, because the earth is not protected by the rains of heaven, and there will be neither dew nor moisture of the air upon the earth. But those who wander through the deserts, fleeing from the face of the serpent[u], bend their knees to God, just as lambs to the udders of their mothers, being sustained by the salvation of the Lord, and while wandering in states of desertion, they eat herbs.

9 Enoch and Elijah

Then, when this inevitability has overwhelmed all people, just and unjust, the just, so that they may be found good by their Lord; and indeed the unjust, so that they may be damned forever with their author the Devil, and, as God beholds the human race in danger and being tossed about by the breath of the horrible dragon, he sends to them consolatory proclamation by his attendants, the prophets Enoch and Elijah, who, while not yet tasting death, are the

---

[t] Mark of the Beast; Revelation 13:16-17
[u] Revelation 12:6

servants for the heralding of the second coming of Christ, and in order to accuse the enemy. And when those just ones have appeared, they confuse indeed the antagonistic serpent with his cleverness and they call back the faithful witnesses to God, in order to (free them) from his seduction ...

10 The Second Coming

And when the three-and-a-half years have been completed, the time of the Antichrist, through which he will have seduced the world, after the resurrection of the two prophets, in the hour which the world does not know, and on the day which the enemy of the son of perdition does not know, will come the sign of the Son of Man. And coming forward, the Lord shall appear with great power and much majesty, with the sign of the wood [the cross] of salvation going before Him, and also even with all the powers of the heavens, with the whole chorus of the saints, with those who bear the sign of the holy cross upon their shoulders, as the angelic trumpet precedes Him, which shall sound and declare: Arise, O sleeping ones, arise, meet Christ, because His hour of judgment has come! Then Christ shall come and the enemy shall be thrown into confusion, and the Lord shall destroy him by the spirit of His mouth. And he shall be bound and shall be plunged into the abyss of everlasting fire, alive, with his father Satan; and all people, who do his wishes, shall perish with him forever; but the righteous ones shall inherit everlasting life with the Lord forever and ever.

The End Times - Ephrem

Summary of *The End Times*

Ephrem agrees with the information previously given but also states that those who are ignorant of the prophecies need to repent of that sin. He correctly saw, not only the division of the Roman Empire, but the division by two brothers and the eastern half creating a Christian empire and its fall (which occurred in AD 1453). He agrees with Irenaeus on a pre-trib rapture. He, like the rest of the fathers, taught the two witnesses would be literally Enoch and Elijah physically returning to earth; or, as John the Baptist came in the spirit and power of Elijah, so two modern Jews will be anointed in the spirit and power of Enoch and Elijah. Either way, the two witnesses are consistently referred to as Enoch and Elijah. Between Ephrem and Hippolytus we come to understand that the Antichrist being born "of the tribe of Dan" means in the tribal area of Dan to the north, or in the Golan area.

Notable Points
- Ephrem connects the Psalm 83 prophecy with the reign of the Antichrist. Ephrem's interpretation of Edom, Moab, and Ammon escaping out of the Antichrist's hand (Daniel 11:41) is that they are the first to surrender, and therefore avoid slaughter (Psalm 83:8).
- He connects Daniel's prophecy of the Antichrist "not regarding the desire of women" with a reinstitution of mandatory circumcision laws in Israel.

The End Times by the Ancient Church Fathers

Ephrem's End-Time Outline

1. Nation of Israel dissolved (AD 132)
2. Roman Empire divided (AD 395) [1b]
3. Christian Byzantine Empire forms (AD 395) [5a]
4. Western Roman Empire dissolved (AD 476)
5. Byzantine-Persian Wars (AD 602-628) [1b]
6. Christian Byzantine Empire overtaken (AD 1453)
7. Desert peoples become warlike (senseless) [3]
8. Antichrist born in the Golan [5b-6]
9. Worthless ten nations arise [4]

Seven Years Begin
10. Rapture of the Church [2]
11. Antichrist craftily takes the kingdom [6]
12. Antichrist appeases the Jews by reinstituting circumcision [7]
13. Enoch and Elijah testify 1260 days [9]
14. Antichrist wars – Ps. 83 [7]
15. People hide in the rocks from the wars [4]
16. Ammon and Moab surrender to Antichrist first [7]

Middle of the Seven Years
17. Antichrist slays the two witnesses
18. Temple sacrifices stopped
19. Abomination set up in temple [7]
20. Mark of the beast implemented [8]

End of the Seven years
21. Second Coming of Messiah [10]
22. Destruction of Antichrist and his kingdom [10]

23. Christ's millennial kingdom established [10]

Hippolytus' *The Antichrist*

Treatise on Christ and Antichrist

1-4 General Introduction

Since you, my beloved brother Theophilus, desired to be thoroughly informed on those topics which I summarized to you, it seemed only right to clarify them for you, drawing mainly from the Holy Scriptures themselves as from a holy fountain, in order that you may not only have the pleasure of hearing them on the testimony of men, but may also be able, by studying them in the light of divine authority, to glorify God in all. For this will be as a sure supply furnished you by us for your journey in this present life, so that by ready argument, applying things ill understood, and apprehended by most, you may sow them in the ground of your heart, as in a rich and clean soil. By these, too, you will be able to silence those who oppose and gainsay the Word of salvation. Only see that you do not give these things over to unbelieving and blasphemous tongues, for that is no common danger. But impart them to pious and faithful men, who desire to live holily and righteously with fear. For it is not to no purpose that the blessed apostle exhorts Timothy, and says,

> "O Timothy, keep that which is committed to thy trust, avoiding profane and vain babblings, and oppositions of science falsely so called; which

some professing have erred concerning the faith."
1 Timothy 6:20-21

And again,
> "Thou therefore, my son, be strong in the grace that is in Christ Jesus. And the things that thou hast heard of me in many exhortations, the same commit thou to faithful men, who shall be able to teach others also." *2 Timothy 2:1-2*

If, then, the blessed apostle delivered these things with a pious caution, which could be easily known by all, as he perceived in the spirit that

> "all men have not faith," *2 Thessalonians 3:2*

how much greater will be our danger, if, rashly and without thought, we commit the revelations of God to profane and unworthy men?[v]

2. General Introduction, Continued

For as the blessed prophets were made, so to speak, eyes for us, they foresaw through faith the mysteries of the Word, and became ministers of these things also to succeeding generations, not only reporting the past, but also announcing the present and the future, so that the prophet might not appear to be one only for the time being, but might also predict the future for all generations, and so be reckoned a true prophet. For these fathers were

---

[v] If pastors cannot teach prophecy, they will be thought of as fools and the faith will be despised.

The End Times by the Ancient Church Fathers

furnished with the Spirit, and largely honored by the Word Himself; and just as it is with instruments of music, so had they the Word always, like the plectrum, in union with them, and when moved by Him the prophets announced what God willed. For they spake not of their own power[w] (let there be no mistake as to that), neither did they declare what pleased themselves. But first of all they were endowed with wisdom by the Word, and then again were rightly instructed in the future by means of visions. And then, when thus themselves fully convinced, they spake those things which were revealed by God to them alone, and concealed from all others. For with what reason should the prophet be called a prophet, unless he in spirit foresaw the future? For if the prophet spake of any chance event, he would not be a prophet then in speaking of things which were under the eye of all. But one who sets forth in detail things yet to be, was rightly judged a prophet. Wherefore prophets were with good reason called from the very first "seers.[x]" And hence we, too, who are rightly instructed in what was declared aforetime by them, speak not of our own capacity. For we do not attempt to make any change one way or another among ourselves in the words that were spoken of old by them, but we make the Scriptures in which these are written public, and read them to those who can believe rightly; for that is a common benefit for both parties: for him who speaks, in holding in memory and setting forth correctly things uttered of old; and for him who hears, in giving attention to the things spoken. Since, then, in this there is

---

[w] 2 Peter 1:21
[x] 1 Samuel 9:9

a work assigned to both parties together, viz., to him who speaks, that he speaks forth faithfully without regard to risk, and to him who hears, that he hears and receives in faith that which is spoken, I beseech you to strive together with me in prayer to God.

3. General Introduction, Continued

Do you wish then to know in what manner the Word of God, who was again the Son of God, as He was of old the Word, communicated His revelations to the blessed prophets in former times? Well, as the Word shows His compassion and His denial of all respect of persons by all the saints, He enlightens them and adapts them to that which is advantageous for us, like a skillful physician, understanding the weakness of men. And the ignorant He loves to teach, and the erring He turns again to His own true way. And by those who live by faith He is easily found; and to those of pure eye and holy heart, who desire to knock at the door, He opens immediately. For He casts away none of His servants as unworthy of the divine mysteries. He does not esteem the rich man more highly than the poor, nor does He despise the poor man for his poverty. He does not disdain the barbarian, nor does He set the eunuch aside as no man.[y] He does not hate the female on account of the woman's act of disobedience in the beginning, nor does He reject the male on account of the man's transgression. But He seeks all, and desires to save all, wishing to make all the children of God, and calling all the saints unto one perfect man. For there is

---

[y] Isaiah 56:3-5

also one Son or Servant of God, by whom we too, receiving the regeneration through the Holy Spirit, desire to come all unto one perfect and heavenly man.[z]

4. General Introduction, Continued

For whereas the Word of God was without flesh, He took upon Himself the holy flesh by the holy virgin, and prepared a robe which He wove for Himself, like a bridegroom, in the sufferings of the cross, in order that by uniting His own power with our moral body, and by mixing the incorruptible with the corruptible, and the strong with the weak, He might save perishing man. The web-beam, therefore, is the passion of the Lord upon the cross, and the warp on it is the power of the Holy Spirit, and the woof is the holy flesh wrought woven by the Spirit, and the thread is the grace which by the love of Christ binds and unites the two in one, and the combs or rods are the Word; and the workers are the patriarchs and prophets who weave the fair, long, perfect tunic for Christ; and the Word passing through these, like the combs or rods, completes through them that which His Father wills.

5 Prophecy Introduction

Now we must consider the question at hand, letting the previous introduction suffice. We must find out what the Holy Scriptures teach about:
- the occasion and time of the coming of Antichrist
- what tribe he comes from

---

[z] Ephesians 4:13

The Antichrist - Hippolytus

- what his name is (from the number 666 in Scripture)
- how he shall work error among the people, gathering them from the ends of the earth
- his tribulation and persecution against the saints
- how he glorifies himself as God
- what his end shall be
- the Lord's sudden appearing revealed from heaven
- the conflagration of the whole world
- the glorious and heavenly kingdom of the saints
- when they reign together with Christ
- the punishment of the wicked by fire

6 Symbols of the Christ and Antichrist

Now, as our Lord Jesus Christ, who is also God, was prophesied of under the figure of a lion[aa], on account of His royalty and glory, in the same way have the Scriptures also aforetime spoken of Antichrist as a lion, on account of his tyranny and violence. For the deceiver seeks to liken himself in all things to the Son of God. Christ is a lion, so Antichrist is also a lion; Christ is a king, so Antichrist is also a king. The Savior was manifested as a lamb; so he too, in like manner, will appear as a lamb, though within he is a wolf. The Savior came into the World in the circumcision, and he will come in the same manner. The Lord sent apostles among all the nations, and he in like manner will send false apostles. The Savior gathered together the sheep that were scattered abroad, and he in like manner will bring together a people that is scattered abroad. The Lord gave a seal to

---

[aa] Revelation 5:5

those who believed on Him, and he will give one in like manner. The Savior appeared in the form of man, and he too will come in the form of a man. The Savior raised up and showed His holy flesh like a temple, and he will raise a temple of stone in Jerusalem. And his seductive arts we shall exhibit in what follows. But for the present let us turn to the question in hand.

7 Messiah from Judah
Now the blessed Jacob speaks to the following effect in his benedictions, testifying prophetically of our Lord and Savior:

> "Judah, let thy brethren praise thee: thy hand shall be on the neck of thine enemies; thy father's children shall bow down before thee. Judah is a lion's whelp: from the shoot, my son, thou art gone up: he stooped down, he couched as a lion, and as a lion's whelp; who shall rouse him up? A ruler shall not depart from Judah, nor a leader from his thighs, until he come for whom it is reserved; and he shall be the expectation of the nations. Binding his ass to a vine, and his ass's colt to the vine tendril; he shall wash his garment in wine, and his clothes in the blood of the grapes. His eyes shall be gladsome as with wine, and his teeth shall be whiter than milk." *Genesis 49:8-12*

8 Messiah Resurrects After Three Days
Knowing, then, as I do, how to explain these things in detail, I deem it right at present to quote the words

The Antichrist - Hippolytus

themselves. But since the expressions themselves urge us to speak of them, I shall not omit to do so. For these are truly divine and glorious things, and things well calculated to benefit the soul. The prophet, in using the expression, "a lion's whelp," means Him who sprang from Judah and David according to the flesh, who was not made indeed of the seed of David, but was conceived by the Holy Ghost, and came forth from the holy shoot of earth. For Isaiah says,

> "There shall come forth a rod out of the root of Jesse, and a flower shall grow up out of it."
> *Isaiah 11:1*

That which is called by Isaiah a flower[bb], Jacob calls a shoot. For first he shot forth, and then he flourished in the world. And the expression, "he stooped down, he couched as a lion, and as a lion's whelp," refers to the three days' sleep (death, couching) of Christ; as also Isaiah says,

> "How is faithful Sion become an harlot![cc] it was full of judgment; in which righteousness lodged (couched); but now murderers." *Isaiah 1:21*

And David says to the same effect,

> "I laid me down (couched) and slept; I awaked: for the Lord will sustain me;" *Psalm 3:5*

[bb] Flower is from LXX; Heb. has Branch.
[cc] I wonder if he is trying to say at one time Jerusalem was the Babylonian harlot?

in which words he points to the fact of his sleep and rising again. And Jacob says, "Who shall rouse him up?" And that is just what David and Paul both refer to, as when Paul says,

> "and God the Father, who raised Him from the dead." *Galatians 1:1*

9 Messiah a Descendant of David
And in saying, "A ruler shall not depart from Judah, nor a leader from his thighs, until he come for whom it is reserved; and he shall be the expectation of the nations," he referred to the fulfilment of that prophecy to Christ. For He is our expectation. For we expect Him, and by faith we behold Him as He comes from heaven with power.

10 The Jews and Gentiles in One Faith
"Binding his ass to a vine:" that means that He unites His people of the circumcision with His own calling vocation, for He was the vine. "And his ass's colt to the vine-tendril" that denotes the people of the Gentiles, as He calls the circumcision and the uncircumcision unto one faith.

11 Messiah's atoning Death
"He shall wash his garment in wine," that is, according to that voice of His Father which came down by the Holy Ghost at the Jordan. "And his clothes in the blood of the grape." In the blood of what grape, then, but just His own flesh, which hung upon the tree like a cluster of grapes? –

from whose side also flowed two streams, of blood and water, in which the nations are washed and purified, which nations He may be supposed to have as a robe about Him.

12 Messiah Testified by the Prophets
"His eyes gladsome with wine." And what are the eyes of Christ but the blessed prophets, who foresaw in the Spirit, and announced beforehand, the sufferings that were to befall Him, and rejoiced in seeing Him in power with spiritual eyes, being furnished for their vocation by the Word Himself and His grace?

13 Messiah's Commands Are Pure
And in saying, "And his teeth shall be whiter than milk," he referred to the commandments that proceed from the holy mouth of Christ, and which are pure, purify as milk.

14 Antichrist from the Tribe of Dan
Thus did the Scriptures preach before-time of this lion and lion's whelp. And in like manner also we find it written regarding Antichrist. For Moses speaks thus:

> "Dan is a lion's whelp, and he shall leap from Bashan." *Deuteronomy 33:22*

But that no one may err by supposing that this is said of the Savior, let him attend carefully to the matter. "Dan," he says, "is a lion's whelp;" and in naming the tribe of Dan, he declared clearly the tribe from which Antichrist is destined to spring. For as Christ springs from the tribe of

Judah, so Antichrist is to spring from the tribe of Dan. And that the case stands thus, we see also from the words of Jacob:

> "Let Dan be a serpent, lying upon the ground, biting the horse's heel." *Genesis 49:17*

What, then, is meant by the serpent but Antichrist, that deceiver who is mentioned in Genesis, [3:1] who deceived Eve and bruised Adam's heel? But since it is necessary to prove this assertion by sufficient testimony, we shall not shrink from the task.

15 No Jewish King Came from the Tribe of Dan

That it is in reality out of the tribe of Dan, then, that that tyrant and king, that dread judge, that son of the devil, is destined to spring and arise, the prophet testifies when he says,

> "Dan shall judge his people, as he is also one tribe in Israel." *Genesis 49:16*

But someone may say that this refers to Samson, who sprang from the tribe of Dan, and judged the people twenty years. Well, the prophecy had its partial fulfilment in Samson, but its complete fulfilment is reserved for Antichrist. For Jeremiah also speaks to this effect:

> "From Dan we are to hear the sound of the swiftness of his horses: the whole land trembled at

the sound of the neighing, of the driving of his horses." *Jeremiah 8:16*

And another prophet says:

"He shall gather together all his strength, from the east even to the west. They whom he calls, and they whom he calls not, shall go with him. He shall make the sea white with the sails of his ships, and the plain black with the shields of his armaments. And whosoever shall oppose him in war shall fall by the sword." *Unknown verse*

That these things, then, are said of no one else but that tyrant, and shameless one, and adversary of God, we shall show in what follows.

16 Antichrist called the Assyrian – Isaiah 10
But Isaiah also speaks thus:

"And it shall come to pass, that when the Lord hath performed His whole work upon Mount Zion and on Jerusalem, He will punish (visit) the stout mind, the king of Assyria, and the greatness (height) of the glory of his eyes. For he said, By my strength will I do it, and by the wisdom of my understanding I will remove the bounds of the peoples, and will rob them of their strength: and I will make the inhabited cities tremble, and will gather the whole world in my hand like a nest, and I will lift it up like eggs that are left. And there is no one that shall escape or gainsay me, and open the mouth and chatter. Shall the axe boast itself without him that heweth therewith? or shall the saw magnify itself without him that shaketh (draweth) it? As if one should raise a rod or a staff, and the staff should lift itself up: and not thus. But the Lord shall send dishonor unto thy honor; and into thy glory a burning fire shall burn. And the light of Israel shall be a fire, and shall sanctify him in flame, and shall consume the forest like grass." *Isaiah 10:12-17*

17 Antichrist – Isaiah 14

And again he says in another place:

"How hath the exactor ceased, and how hath the oppressor ceased! God hath broken the yoke of the rulers of sinners, He who smote the people in wrath, and with an incurable stroke: He that strikes the people with an incurable stroke, which He did not spare. He ceased (rested) confidently: the whole earth shouts with rejoicing. The trees of Lebanon rejoiced at thee, and the cedar of Lebanon, saying, Since thou art laid down, no feller is come up against us. Hell from beneath is moved at meeting thee: all the mighty ones, the rulers of the earth, are gathered together – the lords from their thrones. All the kings of the nations, all they shall answer together, and shall say, And thou, too, art taken as we; and thou art reckoned among us. Thy pomp is brought down to earth, thy great rejoicing: they will spread decay under thee; and the worm shall be thy covering. How art thou fallen from heaven, O Lucifer, son of the morning! He is cast down to the ground who sends off to all the nations. And thou didst say in thy mind, I will ascend into heaven, I will set my throne above the stars of heaven: I will sit down upon the lofty mountains towards the north: I will ascend above the clouds: I will be like the Most High. Yet now thou shalt be brought down to hell, and to the foundations of the earth! They that see thee shall wonder at thee, and shall say, This is the man that excited the earth, that did shake kings, that made the whole world a wilderness, and destroyed the cities, that released not those in prison. All the kings of the earth did lie in honor, everyone in his own house; but thou shall be cast out on the mountains like a loathsome carcass, with many who fall, pierced through with the sword, and going down to hell. As a garment stained with blood is not pure, so neither shall thou be comely (or clean); because thou hast destroyed my land, and slain my people. Thou shalt not abide, enduring forever, a wicked seed. Prepare thy children for slaughter, for the sins of thy father, that they rise not, neither possess my land." *Isaiah 14:4-21*[dd]

[dd] Isaiah 14:24-28 tells of the destruction of Assyria.

18 Antichrist – Ezekiel 28

Ezekiel also speaks of him to the same effect, thus:

> "Thus saith the Lord God, Because thine heart is lifted up, and thou hast said, I am God, I sit in the seat of God, in the midst of the sea; yet art thou a man, and not God, though thou hast set thine heart as the heart of God. Art thou wiser than Daniel? Have the wise not instructed thee in their wisdom? With thy wisdom or with thine understanding hast thou gotten thee power, and gold and silver in thy treasures? By thy great wisdom and by thy traffic hast thou increased thy power? Thy heart is lifted up in thy power. Therefore, thus saith the Lord God: Because thou hast set thine heart as the heart of God: behold, therefore I will bring strangers upon thee, plagues from the nations: and they shall draw their swords against thee, and against the beauty of thy wisdom; and they shall level thy beauty to destruction; and they shall bring thee down; and thou shall die by the death of the wounded in the midst of the sea. Wilt thou yet say before them that slay thee, I am God? But thou art a man, and no God, in the hand of them that wound thee. Thou shalt die the deaths of the uncircumcised by the hand of strangers: for I have spoken it, saith the Lord." *Ezekiel 28:2-10*

19 Nebuchadnezzar's Image

These words then being thus presented, let us observe somewhat in detail what Daniel says in his visions. For in distinguishing the kingdoms that are to rise after these things, he showed also the coming of Antichrist in the last times, and the consummation of the whole world. In expounding the vision of Nebuchadnezzar, then, he speaks thus:

> "Thou, O king, sawest, and behold a great image standing before thy face: the head of which was of fine gold, its arms and shoulders of silver, its belly and its thighs of brass, and its legs of iron, and its feet part of iron and part of clay. Thou sawest, then, till that a stone was cut out without hands, and smote the image upon the feet that were of iron and clay, and brake them to an end. Then were the clay, the iron, the brass, the silver, and the gold broken, and became like the chaff from the summer threshing-floor; and the strength (fullness) of the wind carried them away, and there was no place found for them. And the stone that smote the image became a great mountain, and filled the whole earth." *Daniel 2:31-35*

20 Daniel's Beast Vision

Now if we set Daniel's own visions also side-by-side with this, we shall have one exposition to give of the two together, and shall be able to show how concordant with each other they are, and how true. For he speaks thus:

"I Daniel saw, and behold the four winds of the heaven strove upon the great sea. And four great beasts came up from the sea, diverse one from another. The first was like a lioness, and had wings as of an eagle. I beheld till the wings thereof were plucked, and it was lifted up from the earth, and made stand upon the feet as a man, and a man's heart was given to it. And behold a second beast like to a bear, and it was made stand on one part, and it had three ribs in the mouth of it. I beheld, and lo a beast like a leopard, and it had upon the back of it four wings of a fowl, and the beast had four heads. After this I saw, and behold a fourth beast, dreadful and terrible, and strong exceedingly; it had iron teeth *and claws of brass*, which devoured and brake in pieces, and it stamped the residue with the feet of it; and it was diverse from all the beasts that were before it, and it had ten horns. I considered its horns, and behold there came up among them another little horn, and before it there were three of the first horns plucked up by the roots; and behold in this horn were eyes like the eyes of man, and a mouth speaking great things." *Daniel 7:2-8*

21 The Judgment of the Beast

"I beheld till the thrones were set, and the Ancient of days did sit: and His garment was white as snow, and the hair of His head like pure wool: His throne was a flame of fire, His wheels were a burning fire. A stream of fire flowed before Him.

Thousand thousands ministered unto Him, and ten thousand times ten thousand stood around Him: the judgment was set, and the books were opened. I beheld then, because of the voice of the great words which the horn spake, till the beast was slain and perished, and his body given to the burning of fire. And the dominion of the other beasts was taken away." *Daniel 7:9-12*

22 Daniel's Vision of Messiah
"I saw in the night vision, and, behold, one like the Son of man was coming with the clouds of heaven, and came to the Ancient of days, and was brought near before Him. And there was given Him dominion, and honor, and the kingdom; and all peoples, tribes, and tongues shall serve Him: His dominion is an everlasting dominion, which shall not pass away, and His kingdom shall not be destroyed." *Daniel 7:13-14*

23 Daniel's Winged Lion – Babylon
Now since these things, spoken as they are with a mystical meaning, may seem to some hard to understand, we shall keep back nothing fitted to impart an intelligent apprehension of them to those who are possessed of a sound mind. He said, then, that a "lioness came up from the sea," and by that he meant the kingdom of the Babylonians in the world, which also was the head of gold on the image. In saying that "it had wings as of an eagle," he meant that Nebuchadnezzar the king was lifted up and was exalted against God. Then he says, "the wings

thereof were plucked," that is to say, his glory was destroyed; for he was driven out of his kingdom. And the words, "a man's heart was given to it, and it was made stand upon the feet as a man," refer to the fact that he repented and recognized himself to be only a man, and gave the glory to God.

24a Daniel's Bear – Medo-Persia

Then, after the lioness, he sees a "second beast like a bear," and that denoted the Persians. For after the Babylonians, the Persians held the sovereign power and in saying that there were "three ribs in the mouth of it," he pointed to three nations, viz., the Persians, and the Medes, and the Babylonians; which were also represented on the image by the silver after the gold.

24b Daniel's Leopard – Greece

Then (there was) "the third beast, a leopard," which meant the Greeks. For after the Persians, Alexander of Macedon obtained the sovereign power on subverting Darius, as is also shown by the brass on the image. And in saying that it had "four wings of a fowl," he taught us most clearly how the kingdom of Alexander was partitioned. For in speaking of "four heads," he made mention of four kings, viz., those who arose out of that kingdom. For Alexander, when dying, partitioned out his kingdom into four divisions.

25a Daniel's Non-Descript Beast – Rome

Then he says: "A fourth beast, dreadful and terrible; it had iron teeth and claws of brass." And who are these but the

Romans? Which kingdom is meant by the iron – the kingdom which is now established; for the legs of that image were of iron.

25b Ten Toes / Horns

And after this, what remains, beloved, but the toes of the feet of the image, in which part is iron and part clay, mixed together? And mystically by the toes of the feet he meant the kings who are to arise from among them; as Daniel also says in these words, "I considered the beast, and lo there were ten horns behind it, among which shall rise another horn, an offshoot, and shall pluck up by the roots the three that were before it." And under this was signified none other than Antichrist, who is also himself to raise the kingdom of the Jews.

25c Three Kingdoms Against the Antichrist

He says that three horns are plucked up by the root by him, viz., the three kings of Egypt, and Libya, and Ethiopia[ee], whom he cuts off in the array of battle. And he, after gaining terrible power over all, being nevertheless a tyrant, shall stir up tribulation and persecution against men, exalting himself against them. For Daniel says:

> "I considered the horn, and behold that horn made war with the saints, and prevailed against them... till the beast was slain and perished, and its body was given to the burning of fire." *Daniel 7:21,11*

[ee] Modern-day Sudan

The End Times by the Ancient Church Fathers

26 The Stone – Messianic Kingdom

After a little space the stone [Dan. 2:34, 45] will come from heaven which smites the image and breaks it in pieces, and subverts all the kingdoms, and gives the kingdom to the saints of the Most High. This is the stone which becomes a great mountain, and fills the whole earth, of which Daniel says:

> "I saw in the night visions, and behold one like the Son of man came with the clouds of heaven, and came to the Ancient of days, and was brought near before Him. And there was given Him dominion, and glory, and a kingdom; and all peoples, tribes, and languages shall serve Him: and His dominion is an everlasting dominion, which shall not pass away, and His kingdom shall not be destroyed." *Daniel 7:13-14*

He showed all power given by the Father to the Son, [Matt. 28:18] who is ordained Lord of things in heaven, and things on earth, and things under the earth, and Judge of all: [Phil. 2:10] of things in heaven, because He was born, the Word of God, before all ages; and of things on earth, because He became man in the midst of men, to re-create our Adam through Himself; and of things under the earth, because He was also reckoned among the dead, preaching the Gospel to the souls of the saints, [1 Pet. 3:19] and by death overcoming death.

27 Future Ten Kingdoms
As these things, then, are in the future, and as the ten toes of the image are equivalent to so many democracies, and the ten horns of the fourth beast are distributed over ten kingdoms, let us look at the subject a little more closely, and consider these matters as in the clear light of a personal survey.

28 Summary of the Image and Daniel's Beasts
The golden head of the image and the lioness denoted the Babylonians; the shoulders and arms of silver, and the bear, represented the Persians and Medes; the belly and thighs of brass, and the leopard, meant the Greeks, who held the sovereignty from Alexander's time; the legs of iron, and the beast dreadful and terrible, expressed the Romans, who hold the sovereignty at present; the toes of the feet which were part clay and part iron, and the ten horns, were emblems of the kingdoms that are yet to rise; the other little horn that grows up among them meant the Antichrist in their midst; the stone that smites the earth and brings judgment upon the world was Christ.

29 We Should Reveal the Mysteries
These things, beloved, we impart to you with fear, and yet readily, on account of the love of Christ, which surpasses all. For if the blessed prophets who preceded us did not choose to proclaim these things, though they knew them, openly and boldly, lest they should disquiet the souls of men, but recounted them mystically in parables and dark sayings, speaking thus,

The End Times by the Ancient Church Fathers

> "Here is the mind which hath wisdom,"
> *Revelation 17:9*

how much greater risk shall we run in venturing to declare openly things spoken by them in obscure terms! Let us look, therefore, at the things which are to befall this unclean harlot in the last days; and let us consider what and what manner of tribulation is destined to visit her in the wrath of God before the judgment, as an earnest of her doom.

30 Jerusalem Literally Destroyed

Come, then, O blessed Isaiah; arise, tell us clearly what thou didst prophesy with respect to the mighty Babylon. For thou didst speak also of Jerusalem, and thy word is accomplished. For thou didst speak boldly and openly:

> "Your country is desolate, your cities are burned with fire; your land, strangers devour it in your presence, and it is desolate as overthrown by many strangers. The daughter of Sion shall be left as a cottage in a vineyard, and as a lodge in a garden of cucumbers, as a besieged city."
> *Isaiah 1:7-8*

What then? Are not these things come to pass? Are not the things announced by thee fulfilled? Is not their country, Judea, desolate? Is not the holy place burned with fire? Are not their walls cast down? Are not their cities destroyed? Their land, do not strangers devour it? Do not the Romans rule the country? And indeed these impious people hated thee, and did saw thee asunder, and they crucified Christ. Thou art dead in the world, but you live in Christ.

31 Many Spoke of Her

Which of you, then, shall I esteem more than thee? Yet Jeremiah, too, is stoned. But if I should esteem Jeremiah most, yet Daniel, too, has his testimony. Daniel, I commend thee above all; yet John, too, gives no false witness. With how many mouths and tongues would I praise you; or rather the Word who spake in you! Ye died with Christ; and ye will live with Christ. Hear ye, and rejoice; behold the things announced by you have been fulfilled in their time. For ye saw these things yourselves first, and then ye proclaimed them to all generations. Ye ministered the oracles of God to all generations. Ye prophets were called, that ye might be able to save all. For then is one a prophet indeed, when, having announced beforetime things about to be, he can afterwards show that they have actually happened. Ye were the disciples of a good Master. These words I address to you as if alive, and with propriety. For ye hold already the crown of life and immortality which is laid up for you in heaven. [2 Tim. 4:8]

32 The Accuracy of Daniel

Speak with me, O blessed Daniel. Give me full assurance, I beseech thee. You prophesied concerning the lioness in Babylon; [Daniel 7:4] for you were a captive there. You unfolded the future regarding the bear; for you were still living, and saw the things come to pass. Then you spoke to me of the leopard; and how could you have known this, for you had already died? Who instructed you to announce these things, but He who formed you in your mother's womb? That is God, you said. You spoke the truth and did not lie. The leopard has arisen; the he-goat is come; he hath smitten the ram; he hath broken his horns in pieces; he hath stamped upon him with his feet. He has been exalted by his fall; (the) four horns have come up from under that one [Dan. 8:2-8]. Rejoice, blessed Daniel! you were not wrong: all these things have come to pass.

33 Rome Still Rules –
After this again you spoke of the beast dreadful and terrible.

> "It had iron teeth and claws of brass: it devoured and brake in pieces, and stamped the residue with the feet of it." *Daniel 7:7*

Already the iron rules; already it subdues and breaks all in pieces; already it brings all the unwilling into subjection; already we see these things ourselves. Now we glorify God, being instructed by you.

34-35 The Harlot – Isaiah
But as the task before us was to speak of the harlot, let us mark what the blessed Isaiah said about Babylon.

> "Come down, sit upon the ground, O virgin daughter of Babylon; sit, O daughter of the Chaldeans; thou shalt no longer be called tender

and delicate. Take the millstone, grind meal, draw aside thy veil, shave the grey hairs, make bare the legs, pass over the rivers. Thy shame shall be uncovered, thy reproach shall be seen: I will take justice of thee, I will no more give thee over to men. As for thy Redeemer, He is the Lord of hosts, the Holy One of Israel is His name. Sit thou in compunction, get thee into darkness, O daughter of the Chaldeans: thou shall no longer be called the strength of the kingdom." *Isaiah 47:1-5*

35. The Harlot – Isaiah, Continued

"I was wroth with my people; I have polluted mine inheritance, I have given them into thine hand: and thou didst show them no mercy; but upon the ancient, the elders, thou hast very heavily laid thy yoke. And thou saidst, I shall be a princess forever: thou didst not lay these things to thy heart, neither didst remember thy latter end. Therefore, hear now this, thou that art delicate; that sittest, that art confident, that sayest in thine heart, I am, and there is none else; I shall not sit as a widow, neither shall I know the loss of children. But now these two things shall come upon thee in one day, widowhood and the loss of children: they shall come upon thee suddenly in thy sorcery, in the strength of thine enchantments mightily, in the hope of thy fornication. For thou hast said, I am, and there is none else. And thy fornication shall be thy shame, because thou hast said in thy heart, I am. And destruction shall come upon thee, and

thou shalt not know it. And there shall be a pit, and thou shalt fall into it; and misery shall fall upon thee, and thou shalt not be able to be made clean; and destruction shall come upon thee, and thou shalt not know it. Stand now with thy enchantments, and with the multitude of thy sorceries, which thou hast learned from thy youth; if so be thou shalt be able to be profited. Thou art wearied in thy counsels. Let the astrologers of the heavens stand and save thee; let the star-gazers announce to thee what shall come upon thee. Behold, they shall all be as sticks for the fire; so shall they be burned, and they shall not deliver their soul from the flame. Because thou hast coals of fire, sit upon them; so shall it be for thy help. Thou art wearied with change from thy youth. Man has gone astray each one by himself; and there shall be no salvation for thee."
Isaiah 47:6-15

These things Isaiah prophesied for Babylon. Let us see now whether John predicted these same things.

36-42 The Harlot – Revelation
For he sees, when in the isle Patmos, a revelation of awful mysteries, which he recounts freely, and makes known to others. Tell me, blessed John, apostle and disciple of the Lord, what did you see and hear concerning Babylon? Arise, and speak; for it sent thee also into banishment.

"And there came one of the seven angels which had the seven vials, and talked with me, saying unto me, Come hither; I will show unto thee the judgment of the great whore that sitteth upon many waters; with whom the kings of the earth have committed fornication, and the inhabitants of the earth have been made drunk with the wine of her fornication. And he carried me away in the spirit into the wilderness: and I saw a woman sit upon a scarlet-colored beast, full of names of blasphemy, having seven heads and ten horns. And the woman was arrayed in purple and scarlet color, and decked with gold, and precious stone, and pearls, having a golden cup in her hand, full of abominations and filthiness of the fornication of the earth. Upon her forehead was a name written, Mystery, Babylon the Great, the Mother of Harlots and Abominations of the Earth." *Revelation 17:1-5*

37. "And I saw the woman drunken with the blood of the saints, and with the blood of the martyrs of Jesus: and when I saw her, I wondered with great admiration. And the angel said unto me, Wherefore didst thou marvel? I will tell thee the mystery of the woman, and of the beast that carrieth her, which hath the seven heads and the ten horns. The beast that thou sawest was, and is not; and shall ascend out of the bottomless pit, and go into perdition: and they that dwell on the earth shall wonder whose name was not written in the book of life from the foundation of the world when they behold the beast that was, and is not, and yet shall be." *Revelation 17:6-8*

38. "And here is the mind that has wisdom. The seven heads are seven mountains, on which the woman sitteth. And there are seven kings: five are fallen, and one is, and the other is not yet come; and when he cometh, he must continue a short space. And the beast that was and is not, even he is the eighth, and is of the seven, and goeth into perdition. And the ten horns which thou sawest are ten kings, which have received no kingdom as yet; but receive power as kings one hour with the beast. These have one mind, and shall give their power and strength unto the beast. These shall make war with the Lamb, and the Lamb shall overcome them: for He is Lord of lords, and King of kings; and they that are with Him are called, and chosen, and faithful." *Revelation 17:9-14*

39. "And he saith to me, The waters which thou sawest, where the whore sitteth, are peoples, and multitudes, and nations, and tongues. And the ten horns which thou sawest, and the beast, these shall hate the whore, and shall make her desolate and naked, and shall eat her flesh, and burn her with fire. For God hath put in their hearts to fulfil His will, and to agree, and give their kingdom unto the beast, until the words of God shall be fulfilled. And the woman which thou sawest is

that great city, which reigneth over the kings of the earth." *Revelation 17:15-18*

40. "After these things I saw another angel come down from heaven, having great power; and the earth was lightened with his glory. And he cried mightily with a strong voice, saying, Babylon the great is fallen, is fallen, and is become the habitation of devils, and the hold of every foul spirit, and a cage of every unclean and hateful bird. For all nations have drunk of the wine of the wrath of her fornication, and the kings of the earth have committed fornication with her, and the merchants of the earth are waxed rich through the abundance of her delicacies. And I heard another voice from heaven, saying, Come out of her, my people, that ye be not partakers of her sins, and that ye receive not of her plagues: for her sins did cleave even unto heaven, and God hath remembered her iniquities." *Revelation 18:1-5*

41. "Reward her even as she rewarded you, and double unto her double, according to her works: in the cup which she hath filled, fill to her double. How much she hath glorified herself, and lived deliciously, so much torment and sorrow give her: for she saith in her heart, I sit a queen, and am no widow, and shall see no sorrow. Therefore shall her plagues come in one day, death, and mourning, and famine; and she shall be utterly burned with fire: for strong is the Lord God who

judgeth her. And the kings of the earth, who have committed fornication, and lived deliciously with her, shall bewail her, and lament for her, when they shall see the smoke of her burning, standing afar off for the fear of her torment, saying, Alas, alas! that great city Babylon, that mighty city! for in one hour is thy judgment come. And the merchants of the earth shall weep and mourn over her; for no man shall buy their merchandise any more. The merchandise of gold, and silver, and precious stones, and of pearls, and fine linen, and purple, and silk, and scarlet, and all thine wood, and all manner vessels of ivory, and all manner vessels of most precious wood, and of brass, and iron, and marble, and cinnamon, and spices, and odors, and ointments, and frankincense, and wine, and oil, and fine flour, and wheat, and beasts, and sheep, and goats, and horses, and chariots, and slaves, and souls of men. And the fruits that thy soul lusted after are departed from thee, and all things which were dainty and goodly have perished from thee, and thou shalt find them no more at all. The merchants of these things, which were made rich by her, shall stand afar off for the fear of her torment, weeping and wailing, and saying, Alas, alas! that great city, that was clothed in fine linen, and purple, and scarlet, and decked with gold, and precious stones, and pearls! for in one hour so great riches is come to naught. And every shipmaster, and all the company in ships, and sailors, and as many as trade by sea, stood

The Antichrist - Hippolytus

afar off, and cried, when they saw the smoke of her burning, saying, What city is like unto this great city? And they cast dust on their heads, and cried, weeping and wailing, saying, Alas, alas! that great city, wherein were made rich all that had ships in the sea by reason of her fatness! for in one hour is she made desolate."
Revelation 18:6-19

42. "Rejoice over her, thou heaven, and ye angels, and apostles, and prophets; for God hath avenged you on her. And a mighty angel took up a stone like a great millstone, and cast it into the sea, saying, Thus with violence shall that great city Babylon be thrown down, and shall be found no more at all. And the voice of harpers and musicians, and of pipers and trumpeters, shall be heard no more at all in thee; and no craftsman, of whatsoever craft he be, shall be found any more in thee; and the sound of a millstone shall be heard no more at all in thee; and the light of a candle shall shine no more at all in thee; and the voice of the bridegroom and of the bride shall be heard no more at all in thee: for thy merchants were the great men of the earth; for by thy sorceries were all nations deceived. And in her was found the blood of prophets and of saints, and of all that were slain upon the earth." *Revelation 18:20-24*

43 Summary of the Harlot

With respect, then, to the particular judgment in the torments that are to come upon it in the last times by the hand of the tyrants who shall arise then, the clearest statement has been given in these passages. But it becomes us further diligently to examine and set forth the period at which these things shall come to pass, and how the little horn shall spring up in their midst. For when the legs of iron have issued in the feet and toes, according to the similitude of the image and that of the terrible beast, as has been shown in the above, then shall be the time when the iron and the clay shall be mingled together. Now Daniel will set forth this subject to us. For he says,

> "And one week will make a covenant with many, and it shall be that in the midst of the week my sacrifice and oblation shall cease."
> *Daniel 9:27*

By one week, therefore, he meant the last week which is to be at the end of the whole world, of which week the two prophets Enoch and Elias will take up the half. For they will preach 1,260 days clothed in sackcloth, proclaiming repentance to the people and to all the nations.

44a The Two Advents of Messiah

For as two advents of our Lord and Savior are indicated in the Scriptures, the one being His first advent in the flesh, which took place without honor by reason of His being set at naught, as Isaiah spake of Him aforetime, saying,

The Antichrist - Hippolytus

> "We saw Him, and He had no form nor comeliness, but His form was despised and rejected above all men; a man smitten and familiar with bearing infirmity, for His face was turned away; He was despised, and esteemed not." *Isaiah 53:2-5*

But His second advent is announced as glorious, when He shall come from heaven with the host of angels, and the glory of His Father, as the prophet said,

> "Ye shall see the King in glory;" *Isaiah 33:17*

and,

> "I saw one like the Son of man coming with the clouds of heaven; and he came to the Ancient of days, and he was brought to Him. And there were given Him dominion, and honor, and glory, and the kingdom; all tribes and languages shall serve Him: His dominion is an everlasting dominion, which shall not pass away." *Daniel 7:13-14*

44b-46a The Witness of the First Coming

Thus also two forerunners were indicated. The first was John the son of Zacharias, who appeared in all things a forerunner and herald of our Savior, preaching of the heavenly light that had appeared in the world. He first fulfilled the course of forerunner, and that from his mother's womb, being conceived by Elisabeth, in order that to those, too, who are children from their mother's womb he might declare the new birth that was to take place for their sakes by the Holy Ghost and the Virgin.

45. The Witness of the First Coming, Continued
He, on hearing the salutation addressed to Elisabeth, leaped with joy in his mother's womb, recognizing God the Word conceived in the womb of the Virgin. Thereafter he came forward preaching in the wilderness, proclaiming the baptism of repentance to the people, and thus announcing prophetically salvation to the nations living in the wilderness of the world. After this, at the Jordan, seeing the Savior with his own eye, he points Him out, and says,

> "Behold the Lamb of God, which taketh away the sin of the world!" *John 1:29*

He also first preached to those in Hades, becoming a forerunner there when he was put to death by Herod, that there too he might intimate that the Savior would descend to ransom the souls of the saints from the hand of death.

46. The Witness of the First Coming, Continued
But since the Savior was the beginning of the resurrection of all men, it was meet that the Lord alone should rise from the dead, by whom too the judgment is to enter for the whole world, that they who have wrestled worthily may be also crowned worthily by Him, by the illustrious Arbiter, to wit, who Himself first accomplished the course, and was received into the heavens, and was set

down on the right hand of God the Father, and is to be manifested again at the end of the world as Judge.

46b Second Coming Witnesses
It is a matter of course that His forerunners must appear first, as He says by Malachi and the angel,

> "I will send to you Elias the Tishbite before the day of the Lord, the great and notable day, comes; and he shall turn the hearts of the fathers to the children, and the disobedient to the wisdom of the just, lest I come and smite the earth utterly."
> *Malachi 4:5-6*

These, then, shall come and proclaim the manifestation of Christ that is to be from heaven; and they shall also perform signs and wonders, in order that men may be put to shame and turned to repentance for their surpassing wickedness and impiety.

47 The Timing of the Two Witnesses
For John says,

> "And I will give power unto my two witnesses, and they shall prophesy a thousand two hundred and threescore days, clothed in sackcloth."
> *Revelation 11:3*

That is the half of the week that Daniel spoke about.

The End Times by the Ancient Church Fathers

> "These are the two olive trees and the two candlesticks standing before the Lord of the earth. And if any man will hurt them, fire will proceed out of their mouth, and devour their enemies; and if any man will hurt them, he must in this manner be killed. These have power to shut heaven, that it rain not in the days of their prophecy; and have power over waters, to turn them to blood, and to smite the earth with all plagues as often as they will." *Revelation 11:4-6*

And when they shall have finished their course and their testimony, what does the prophet say?

> "the beast that ascendeth out of the bottomless pit shall make war against them, and shall overcome them, and kill them," *Revelation 11:7*

because they will not give glory to Antichrist. For this is meant by the little horn that grows up. He, being now elated in heart, begins to exalt himself, and to glorify himself as God, persecuting the saints and blaspheming Christ, even as Daniel says,

> "I considered the horns, and, behold, in the horn were eyes like the eyes of man, and a mouth speaking great things; and he opened his mouth to blaspheme God. And that born made war against the saints, and prevailed against them until the beast was slain, and perished, and his body was given to be burned." *Daniel 7:8*

The Antichrist - Hippolytus

48 The Earth Beast

But as it is incumbent on us to discuss this matter of the beast more exactly, and in particular, the question about how the Holy Spirit has also mystically indicated his name by means of a number, we shall proceed to state more clearly what bears upon him. John then speaks thus:

"And I beheld another beast coming up out of the earth; and he had two horns like a lamb, and he spake as a dragon. And he exercised all the power of the first beast before him; and he made the earth and them which dwell therein to worship the first beast, whose deadly wound was healed. And he did great wonders, so that he maketh fire come down from heaven on the earth in the sight of men, and deceiveth them that dwell on the earth by means of those miracles which he had power to do in the sight of the beast, saying to them that dwell on the earth, that they should make an image to the beast which had the wound by a sword and did live. And he had power to give life unto the image of the beast, that the image of the beast should both speak, and cause that as many as would not worship the image of the beast should be killed. And he caused all, both small and great, rich and poor, free and bond, to receive a mark in their right hand or in their forehead; and that no man might buy or sell, save he that had the mark, the name of the beast, or the number of his name. Here is wisdom. Let him that hath understanding count the number of the beast; for if is the number of a man, and his number is six hundred threescore and six." *Revelation 13:11-18*

49 Earth Beast Explained

By the beast, then, coming up out of the earth, he means the kingdom of Antichrist; and by the two horns he means the Antichrist and the false prophet after him. And in speaking of "the horns being like a lamb," he means that he will make himself like the Son of God, and set himself forward as king. And the terms, "he spake like a dragon," mean that he is a deceiver, and not truthful. And the words, "he exercised all the power of the first beast before him, and caused the earth and them which dwell therein to worship the first beast, whose deadly wound was healed," signify that, after the manner of the law of Augustus, by whom the empire of Rome was established, he too will rule and govern, sanctioning everything by it, and taking greater glory to himself. For this is the fourth beast of Daniel, whose head was wounded and healed again, in its being broken up or even dishonored, and partitioned into four crowns[ff]; and he then [the Antichrist] shall with knavish skill heal it, as it were, and restore it. For this is what is meant by the prophet when he says, "He will give life unto the image, and the image of the beast will speak." For he will act with vigor again, and prove strong by reason of the laws established by him; and he will

---

[ff] Either Hippolytus is referring to the Grecian kingdom that was broken into four smaller kingdoms (Greece, Turkey, Syria, and Egypt) or he is referring to the prophecy of the Roman Empire's division from the Ezra apocalypse (the winged empire, and the three heads).

cause all those who will not worship the image of the beast to be put to death. Here the faith and the patience of the saints will appear, for he says: "And he will cause all, both small and great, rich and poor, free and bond, to receive a mark in their right hand or in their forehead; that no man might buy or sell, save he that had the mark, the name of the beast, or the number of his name." For, being full of guile, and exalting himself against the servants of God, with the wish to afflict them and persecute them out of the world, because they give not glory to him, he will order incense-pans to be set up by all everywhere, that no man among the saints may be able to buy or sell without first sacrificing; for this is what is meant by the mark received upon the right hand. And the word – "in their forehead" – indicates that all are crowned, and put on a crown of fire, and not of life, but of death. For in this way, too, did Antiochus Epiphanes, the king of Syria, the descendant of Alexander of Macedon, devise measures against the Jews. He, too, in the exaltation of his heart, issued a decree in those times, that "all should set up shrines before their doors, and sacrifice, and that they should march in procession to the honor of Dionysus, waving chaplets of ivy;" and that those who refused obedience should be put to death by strangulation and torture. But he also met his due recompense at the hand of the Lord, the righteous Judge and all-searching God; for he died eaten up of worms. And if one desires to inquire into that more accurately, he will find it recorded in the books of the Maccabees.

50 The Number of the Beast

But now we shall speak of what is before us. For such measures will he, too, devise, seeking to afflict the saints in every way. For the prophet and apostle says:

> "Here is wisdom, Let him that hath understanding count the number of the beast; for it is the number of a man, and his number is six hundred threescore and six." *Revelation 13:18*

With respect to his name, it is not in our power to explain it exactly, as the blessed John understood it and was instructed about it, but only to give a conjectural account of it; for when he appears, the Blessed One will show us what we seek to know. Yet as far as our doubtful apprehension of the matter goes, we may speak. Many names indeed we find, the letters of which are the equivalent of this number: such as, for instance, the word "Titan," an ancient and notable name; or "Evanthas," for it too makes up the same number; and many others which might be found. But, as we have already said, the wound of the first beast was healed, and he [the second beast] was to make the image speak, that is to say, he should be powerful; and it is manifest to all that those who at present still hold the power are Latins. If, then, we take the name as the name of a single man, it becomes *Latinus*. Wherefore we ought neither to give it out as if this were certainly his name, nor again ignore the fact that he may not be otherwise designated. But having the mystery of God in our heart, we ought in fear to keep faithfully what has been told us by the blessed prophets, in order that when those things come to pass, we may be prepared for them, and not deceived. For when the times advance, he too, of whom these thing are said, will be manifested.

51 Jordan[gg] Falls to the Antichrist

But not to confine ourselves to these words and arguments alone, for the purpose of convincing those who love to study the oracles of God, we shall demonstrate the matter by many other proofs. For Daniel says,

> "And these shall escape out of his hand, even Edom, and Moab, and the chief of the children of Ammon." *Daniel 11:41*

Ammon and Moab[hh] are the children born to Lot by his daughters, and their race survives even now. And Isaiah says:

> "And they shall fly in the boats of strangers, plundering the sea together, and they shall spoil them of the east: and they shall lay hands upon Moab first; and the children of Ammon shall first obey them." *Isaiah 11:14*

52 Tyre and Beirut Fall to the Antichrist

In those times, then, he shall arise and meet them. And when he has overmastered three horns out of the ten in the array of war, and has rooted these out, viz., Egypt, and

---

[gg] Modern Jordan is made up of what used to be the kingdoms of Ammon, Moab, and Edom
[hh] Genesis 19:37-38

The End Times by the Ancient Church Fathers

Libya, and Ethiopia, and has got their spoils and trappings, and has brought the remaining horns which suffer into subjection, he will begin to be lifted up in heart, and to exalt himself against God as master of the whole world. And his first expedition will be against Tyre and Berytus[ii], and the circumjacent territory. For by storming these cities first he will strike terror into the others, as Isaiah says,

> "Be thou ashamed, O Sidon; the sea hath spoken, even the strength of the sea hath spoken, saying, I travailed not, nor brought forth children; neither did I nurse up young men, nor bring up virgins. But when the report comes to Egypt, pain shall seize them for Tyre." *Isaiah 23:4-5*

53 Pride of the Antichrist

These things, then, shall be in the future, beloved; and when the three horns are cut off, he will begin to show himself as God, as Ezekiel has said aforetime:

> "Because thy heart has been lifted up, and thou hast said, I am God." *Ezekiel 28:2*

And to the like effect Isaiah says:

> "For thou hast said in thine heart, I will ascend into heaven, I will exalt my throne above the stars of heaven: I will be like the Most High. Yet now

---

[ii] Berytus is the old name of the city of Beirut, Lebanon.

thou shall be brought down to hell [Hades], to the foundations of the earth." *Isaiah 14:13-15*

In like manner also Ezekiel:

"Wilt thou yet say to those who slay thee, I am God? But thou shall be a man, and no God." *Ezekiel 28:9*

54 Antichrist Gathers His Army

As his tribe, then, and his manifestation, and his destruction, have been set forth in these words, and as his name has also been indicated mystically, let us look also at his action. For he will call together all the people to himself, out of every country of the dispersion, making them his own, as though they were his own children, and promising to restore their country, and establish again their kingdom and nation, in order that he may be worshipped by them as God, as the prophet says: "He will collect his whole kingdom, from the rising of the sun even to its setting: they whom he summons and they whom he does not summon shall march with him." And Jeremiah speaks of him thus in a parable:

"The partridge cried, and gathered what he did not hatch, making himself riches without judgment: in the midst of his days they shall leave him, and at his end he shall be a fool." *Jeremiah 17:11*

55 The Partridge Allegory

It will not be detrimental, therefore, to the course of our present argument, if we explain the art of that creature, and show that the prophet has not spoken without a purpose in using the parable [or similitude] of the creature. For as the partridge is a vainglorious creature, when it sees near at hand the nest of another partridge with young in it, and with the parent-bird away on the wing in quest of food, it imitates the cry of the other bird, and calls the young to itself; and they, taking it to be their own parent, run to it. And it delights itself proudly in the alien pullets as in its own. But when the real parent-bird returns, and calls them with its own familiar cry, the young recognize it, and forsake the deceiver, and betake themselves to the real parent. This thing, then, the prophet has adopted as a simile, applying it in a similar manner to Antichrist. For he will allure mankind to himself, wishing to gain possession of those who are not his own, and promising deliverance to all, while he is unable to save himself.

56 Antichrist's Army Persecutes the Saints

He then, having gathered to himself the unbelieving everywhere throughout the world, comes at their call to persecute the saints[jj], their enemies and antagonists, as the apostle and evangelist says:

> "There was in a city a judge, which feared not God, neither regarded man: and there was a

---

[jj] Muslim call persuades the Antichrist to attack Jews?

widow in that city, who came unto him, saying, Avenge me of mine adversary. And he would not for a while: but afterward he said within himself, Though I fear not God, nor regard man; yet because this widow troubleth me, I will avenge her." *Luke 18:2-5*

57a Luke's Parable Explained

By the unrighteous judge, who fears not God, neither regards man, he means without doubt Antichrist, as he is a son of the devil and a vessel of Satan. For when he has the power, he will begin to exalt himself against God, neither in truth fearing God, nor regarding the Son of God, who is the Judge of all. And in saying that there was a widow in the city, he refers to Jerusalem itself, which is a widow indeed, forsaken of her perfect, heavenly spouse, God. She calls Him her adversary, and not her Savior; for she does not understand that which was said by the prophet Jeremiah:

> "Because they obeyed not the truth, a spirit of error shall speak then to this people and to Jerusalem." *Unknown Verse* [kk]

And Isaiah also to the like effect:

> "Forasmuch as the people refuseth to drink the water of Siloam that goeth softly, but chooseth to

---

[kk] The footnote in *Ante-Nicene Fathers* Vol. 5, p. 216 says this is a quote of Jeremiah 4:11, but it does not match the Hebrew or Septuagint.

have Rasin and Romeliah's son as king over you: therefore, lo, the Lord bringeth up upon you the water of the river, strong and full, even the king of Assyria." *Isaiah 8:6-7*

57b Micah's Assyrian Antichrist

By the king he means metaphorically Antichrist, as also another prophet says:

"And this man shall be the peace from me, when the Assyrian shall come up into your land, and when he shall tread in your mountains."
Micah 5:5

58a Antichrist Uses the Jews

And in like manner, Moses, knowing beforehand that the people would reject and disown the true Savior of the world, and take part with error, and choose an earthly king, and set the heavenly King at naught, says:

"Is not this laid up in store with me, and sealed up among my treasures? In the day of vengeance, I will recompense them, and in the time when their foot shall slide." *Deuteronomy 32:34-35*

They did slide, therefore, in all things, as they were found to be in harmony with the truth in nothing: neither as concerns the law, because they became transgressors; nor as concerns the prophets, because they cut off even the prophets themselves; nor as concerns the voice of the Gospels, because they crucified the Savior Himself; nor in believing the apostles, because they persecuted them. At all times they showed themselves enemies and betrayers of the truth, and were found to be haters of God, and not lovers of Him; and such they shall be then when they find opportunity: for, rousing themselves against the servants of God, they will seek to obtain vengeance by the hand of a mortal man.

58b-59 Antichrist's Ethiopia

And he, being puffed up with pride by their subserviency, will begin to dispatch letters against the saints, commanding to cut them all off everywhere, on the ground of their refusal to reverence and worship him as God, according to the word of Isaiah:

> "Woe to the wings of the vessels of the land, beyond the rivers of Ethiopia: woe to him who sendeth sureties by the sea, and letters of papyrus upon the water; for nimble messengers will go to a nation anxious and expectant, and a people strange and bitter against them; a nation hopeless and trodden down." *Isaiah 18-1-2*

59. Antichrist's Ethiopia, Continued

But we who hope for the Son of God are persecuted and trodden down by those unbelievers. For the wings of the vessels are the churches; and the sea is the world, in which the Church is set, like a ship tossed in the deep, but not destroyed; for she has with her the skilled Pilot, Christ. And she bears in her midst also the trophy which is erected over death; for she carries with her the cross of the Lord. For her prow is the east, and her stern is the west, and her hold is the south, and her tillers are the two Testaments; and the ropes that stretch around her are the love of Christ, which binds the Church; and the net which she bears with her is the laver of the regeneration which renews the believing, whence, too, are these glories. As the wind the Spirit from heaven is present, by whom those who believe are sealed: she has also anchors of iron accompanying her, viz., the holy commandments of Christ Himself, which are strong as iron. She has also mariners on the right and on the left, assessors like the holy angels, by whom the church is always governed and defended. The ladder in her leading up to the sailyard is an emblem of the passion of Christ, which brings the faithful to the ascent of heaven. And the top-sails aloft upon the yard are the company of prophets, martyrs, and apostles, who have entered into their rest in the kingdom of Christ.

60-61 The Sun-clad Woman

Now, concerning the tribulation of the persecution which is to fall upon the Church from the adversary, John also speaks thus:

> "And I saw a great and wondrous sign in heaven; a woman clothed with the sun, and the moon under her feet, and upon her head a crown of twelve stars. And she, being with child, cries, travailing in birth, and pained to be delivered. And the dragon stood before the woman which was ready to be delivered, for to devour her child

as soon as it was born. And she brought forth a man-child, who is to rule all the nations: and the child was caught up unto God and to His throne. And the woman fled into the wilderness, where she hath the place prepared of God, that they should feed her there a thousand two hundred and threescore days. And then when the dragon saw *it*, he persecuted the woman which brought forth the man-*child*. And to the woman were given two wings of the great eagle, that she might fly into the wilderness, where she is nourished for a time, and times, and half a time, from the face of the serpent. And the serpent cast out of his mouth water as a flood after the woman, that he might cause her to be carried away of the flood. And the earth helped the woman, and opened her mouth, and swallowed up the flood which the dragon cast out of his mouth. And the dragon was wroth with the woman, and went to make war with the saints of her seed, which keep the commandments of God, and have the testimony of Jesus."
Revelation 12:1-6

61. The Sun-clad Woman, Continued

By the woman then clothed with the sun," he meant most manifestly the Church[ll], endued with the Father's Word, whose brightness is above the sun. And by the "moon under her feet" he referred to her being adorned, like the moon, with heavenly glory. And the words, "upon her

---

[ll] Those who became believers during the Tribulation.

head a crown of twelve stars," refer to the twelve apostles by whom the Church was founded. And those, "she, being with child, cries, travailing in birth, and pained to be delivered," mean that the Church will not cease to bear from her heart the Word that is persecuted by the unbelieving in the world. "And she brought forth," he says, "a man-child, who is to rule all the nations;" by which is meant that the Church, always bringing forth Christ, the perfect man-child of God, who is declared to be God and man, becomes the instructor of all the nations. And the words, "her child was caught up unto God and to His throne," signify that He who is always born of her is a heavenly king, and not an earthly; even as David also declared of old when he said,

> "The Lord said unto my Lord, Sit Thou at my right hand, until I make Thine enemies Thy footstool." *Psalm 110:1*

> "And the dragon," he says, "saw and persecuted the woman which brought forth the man-child. And to the woman were given two wings of the great eagle, that she might fly into the wilderness, where she is nourished for a time, and times, and half a time, from the face of the serpent." *Revelation 11:13-14*

That refers to the one thousand, two hundred and threescore days [the half of the week] during which the tyrant is to reign and persecute the Church, which flees from city to city, and seeks concealment in the wilderness among the mountains, possessed of no other defense than the two wings of the great eagle, that is to say, the faith of Jesus Christ, who, in stretching forth His holy hands on the holy tree, unfolded two wings, the right and the left, and called to Him all who believed upon Him, and covered them as a hen her chickens. For by the mouth of Malachi also He speaks thus:

> "And unto you that fear My name shall the Sun of righteousness arise with healing in His wings."
> *Malachi 4:2*

62-63 The Abomination of Desolation

The Lord also says,

> "When ye shall see the abomination of desolation stand in the holy place (whoso readeth, let him understand), then let them which be in Judea flee into the mountains, and let him which is on the housetop not come down to take his clothes; neither let him which is in the field return back to take anything out of his house. And woe unto them that are with child, and to them that give suck, in those days! for then shall be great tribulation, such as was not since the beginning of the world. And except those days should be shortened, there should no flesh be saved."
> *Matthew 24:15-22*

And Daniel says,

> "And they shall place the abomination of desolation a thousand two hundred and ninety days. Blessed is he that waiteth, and cometh to the thousand two hundred and ninety-five days."
> *Daniel 12:11*

63. The Abomination of Desolation, Continued

And the blessed apostle Paul, writing to the Thessalonians, says:

> "Now we beseech you, brethren, concerning the coming of our Lord Jesus Christ, and our gathering together at it, that ye be not soon shaken in mind, or be troubled, neither by spirit, nor by word, nor by letters as from us, as that the day of the Lord is at hand. Let no man deceive you by any means; for that day shall not come except there come the falling away first, and that man of sin be revealed, the son of perdition, who opposeth and exalteth himself above all that is called God, or that is worshipped: so that he sitteth in the temple of God, showing himself that he is God. Remember ye not, that when I was yet with you, I told you these things? And now ye know what withholdeth, that he might be revealed in his time. For the mystery of iniquity doth already work; only he who now letteth will let, until he be taken out of the way. And then shall that wicked be revealed, whom the Lord Jesus shall consume with the Spirit of His mouth, and shall destroy with the brightness of His coming:

even him whose coming is after the working of Satan, with all power, and signs, and lying wonders, and with all deceivableness of unrighteousness in them that perish; because they received not the love of the truth. And for this cause God shall send them strong delusion, that they should believe a lie: that they all might be damned who believed not the truth, but had pleasure in unrighteousness."
2 Thessalonians 2:1-11

And Isaiah says,
"Let the wicked be cut off, that he behold not the glory of the Lord." *Isaiah 26:10*

64a The Two Halves of the Tribulation

These things, then, being to come to pass, beloved, and the one week being divided into two parts, and the abomination of desolation being manifested then, and the two prophets and forerunners of the Lord having finished their course, and the whole world finally approaching the consummation, what remains but the coming of our Lord and Savior Jesus Christ from heaven, for whom we have looked in hope? who shall bring the conflagration and just judgment upon all who have refused to believe on Him. For the Lord says,

"And when these things begin to come to pass, then look up, and lift up your heads; for your redemption draweth nigh." *Luke 21:28*

The End Times by the Ancient Church Fathers

> "And there shall not a hair of your head perish."
> *Luke 21:18*

> "For as the lightning cometh out of the east, and shineth even unto the west, so shall also the coming of the Son of man be. For wheresoever the carcass is, there will the eagles be gathered together." *Matthew 24:27-28*

Now the Fall took place in paradise; for Adam fell there. And He says again,

> "Then shall the Son of man send His angels, and they shall gather together His elect from the four winds of heaven." *Matthew 24:31*

And David also, in announcing prophetically the judgment and coming of the Lord, says,

> "His going forth is from the end of the heaven, and His circuit unto the end of the heaven: and there is no one hid from the heat thereof."
> *Psalm 19:6*

64b Pre-Trib Rapture

By the heat he means the conflagration. And Isaiah speaks thus:

> "Come, my people, enter thou into thy chamber, and shut thy door: hide thyself as it were for a

little moment, until the indignation of the Lord be overpast." *Isaiah 26:20*

And Paul in like manner:

> "For the wrath of God is revealed from heaven against all ungodliness and unrighteousness of men, who hold the truth of God in unrighteousness." *Romans 1:18*

65 The Resurrection

Moreover, concerning the resurrection and the kingdom of the saints, Daniel says,

> "And many of them that sleep in the dust of the earth shall arise, some to everlasting life, and some to shame and everlasting contempt."
> *Daniel 12:2*

Isaiah says,

> "The dead men shall arise, and they that are in their tombs shall awake; for the dew from thee is healing to them." *Isaiah 26:19*

The Lord says,

> "Many in that day shall hear the voice of the Son of God, and they that hear shall live." *John 5:25*

And the prophet says,

The End Times by the Ancient Church Fathers

"Awake, thou that sleepest, and arise from the dead, and Christ shall give thee light."
Ephesians 5:14

And John says,
"Blessed and holy is he that hath part in the first resurrection: on such the second death hath no power." *Revelation 20:6*

For the second death is the lake of fire that burns. And again the Lord says,

"Then shall the righteous shine forth as the sun shineth in his glory." *Matthew 13:43*

And to the saints He will say,
"Come, ye blessed of My Father, inherit the kingdom prepared for you from the foundation of the world." *Matthew 25:34*

But what did He say to the wicked?
"Depart from Me, ye cursed, into everlasting fire, prepared for the devil and his angels, which My Father hath prepared." *Matthew 25:41*

And John says,
"Without are dogs, and sorcerers, and whoremongers, and murderers, and idolaters, and whosoever maketh and loveth a lie; for your part is in the hell of fire." *Revelation 22:15*

And in like manner also Isaiah:

> "And they shall go forth and look upon the carcasses of the men that have transgressed against Me. And their worm shall not die, neither shall their fire be quenched; and they shall be for a spectacle to all flesh." *Isaiah 66:24*

66-67 Rapture

Concerning the resurrection of the righteous, Paul also speaks thus in writing to the Thessalonians:

> "We would not have you to be ignorant concerning them which are asleep, that ye sorrow not even as others which have no hope. For if we believe that Jesus died and rose again, even so them also which sleep in Jesus will God bring with Him. For this we say unto you by the word of the Lord, that we which are alive and remain unto the coming of the Lord, shall not prevent them which are asleep. For the Lord Himself shall descend from heaven with a shout, with the voice and trump of God, and the dead in Christ shall rise first. Then we which are alive and remain shall be caught up together with them in the clouds to meet the Lord in the air; and so shall we ever be with the Lord." *1 Thessalonians 4:13-17*

67. Rapture, Continued

These things, then, I have set shortly before you, Theophilus, drawing them from Scripture itself, in order that, maintaining in faith what is written, and anticipating the things that are to be, you may keep yourself void of offence both toward God and toward men,

> "looking for that blessed hope and appearing of our God and Savior," *Titus 2:13*

when, having raised the saints among us, He will rejoice with them, glorifying the Father. To Him be the glory unto the endless ages of the ages. Amen.

Summary of *The Antichrist*

Hippolytus agrees with the teachings of Irenaeus concerning the basic outline of the seven-year tribulation period, what Daniel's visions meant, the Second Coming, and the millennial reign of Christ on earth.

Hippolytus also clarifies some points for us:
- Scripture calls the Antichrist the Assyrian [16, 57].
- The Antichrist's name will equal 666 when spelled out in Greek. Some possible names are: Titan, Evanthas, and Latanus.
- He teaches that Rome was Mystery Babylon in his day [36] but somehow continues to exist past the destruction of the two Roman Empires.
- The ten nations originate out of the area of what used to be the old Roman Empire and what used to be the old Grecian Empire. [49]

- Israel exists today as a democracy. The Antichrist will revive a religious state in Israel.

There might be some replacement theology drifting into the interpretation of prophecy in 58b, about Ethiopia, and chapter 60-61, about the sun-clad woman. These texts do not add any information but treat the subject of prophecy as very symbolic, which is not the case for the rest of the book. This suggests those writings might have been added to or tampered with.

The End Times by the Ancient Church Fathers
Hippolytus' End-Time Outline

1. Jerusalem destroyed by Rome (AD 70) [30]
2. Antichrist born of the circumcision [6]
3. Antichrist born of the tribe of Dan [14-15]
4. Antichrist restores Roman Empire from four pieces. [49]

Seven Years Begin
5. Rapture of the believers [64, 66-67]
6. Antichrist raises up a Jewish kingdom [25b]
7. Antichrist builds the Jerusalem temple [6]
8. Enoch and Elijah witness 1260 days [43,47,64]
9. Antichrist wars begin
10. Jordan submits to Antichrist first [51]
11. Tyre and Beirut, the first to fall to Antichrist [52]
12. Antichrist destroys Egypt, Libya, and Sudan. [25c]
13. The ten nations destroy Babylon [43]

Middle of the Seven Years
14. Temple sacrifices stopped [43]
15. Abomination set up [64], lasts 1290 days [62]
16. Persecution begins

End of the Seven years
17. Millennial reign begins

Hippolytus'
On the End of the World

A Discourse by the Most Blessed Hippolytus, Bishop and Martyr, on the End of the World, and on Antichrist, and on the Second Coming of Our Lord Jesus Christ.

1-2 General Introduction

1 Since, then, the blessed prophets have been eyes to us, setting forth for our benefit the clear declaration of things secret, both through life, and through declaration, and through inspiration of the Holy Spirit, and discoursing, too, of things not yet come to pass, in this way also to all generations they have pictured forth the grandest subjects for contemplation and for action. Thus, too, they preached of the advent of God in the flesh to the world, His advent by the spotless and God-bearing Mary in the way of birth and growth, and the manner of His life and conversation with men, and His manifestation by baptism, and the new birth that was to be to all men, and the regeneration by the laver; and the multitude of His miracles, and His blessed passion on the cross, and the insults which He bore at the hands of the Jews, and His burial, and His descent to Hades, and His ascent again, and redemption of the spirits that were of old, and the destruction of death, and His life-giving awaking from the dead, and His re-creation of the whole world, and His assumption and return to heaven, and His reception of the Spirit, of which the apostles were deemed worthy, and again the second coming, that is destined to declare all things. For as being designated seers, they of necessity signified and spake of these things beforetime.

2 General Introduction, Continued

Hence, too, they indicated the day of the consummation to us, and signified beforehand the day of the apostate that is to appear and deceive men at the last times, and the beginning and end of his kingdom, and the advent of the Judge, and the life of the righteous, and the punishment of the sinners, in order that we all, bearing these things in mind day-by-day and hour-by-hour, as children of the Church, might know that

> "not one jot nor one tittle of these things shall fail," *Matthew 5:18*

as the Savior's own word announced. Let all of you, then, of necessity, open the eyes of your hearts and the ears of your soul, and receive the word which we are about to speak. For I shall unfold to you today a narration full of horror and fear, to wit, the account of the consummation, and in particular, of the seduction of the whole world by the enemy and devil; and after these things, the second coming of our Lord Jesus Christ.

3 The Church Shall Apostatize

Where, then, ye friends of Christ, shall I begin? and with what shall I make my commencement, or what shall I expound? and what witness shall I adduce for the things spoken? But let us take those prophets with whom we began this discourse, and adduce them as credible witnesses, to confirm our exposition of the matters discussed; and after them, the teaching, or rather the prophecy, of the apostles, so as to see how throughout the whole world they herald the day of the consummation. Since these, then, have also shown beforetime things not yet come to pass, and have declared the devices and deceits of wicked men, who are destined to be made manifest, come and let us bring forward Isaiah as our first witness, inasmuch as he instructs us in the times of the consummation. What, then, does he say?

> "Your country is desolate, your cities are burned with fire: your land, strangers devour it in your presence: the daughter of Zion shall be left as a cottage in a vineyard, and as a lodge in a garden of cucumbers, as a besieged city." *Isaiah 1:7-8*

You see, beloved, the prophet's illumination, whereby he announced that time so many generations before. For it is not of the Jews that he spake this word of old, nor of the city of Zion, but of the church. For all the prophets have declared Sion to be the bride brought from the nations.

4 Antichrist's Scorching Eastern Wind

Wherefore let us direct our discourse to a second witness. And of what sort is this one? Listen to Hosea, as he speaks thus grandly:

> "In those days the Lord shall bring on a burning wind from the desert against them, and shall make their veins dry, and shall make their springs desolate; and all their goodly vessels shall be spoiled. Because they rose up against God, they shall fall by the sword, and their women with child shall be ripped up." *Hosea 13:15-16*

And what else is this burning wind from the east than the Antichrist that is to destroy and dry up the veins of the waters and the fruits of the trees in his times, because men set their hearts on his works? For which reason he shall indeed destroy them, and they shall serve him in his pollution.

5-6 The Church is left Desolate
Mark the agreement of prophet with prophet. Acquaint yourself also with another prophet who expresses himself in like manner. For Amos prophesied of the same things in a manner quite in accordance:

> "Thus saith the Lord, Forasmuch therefore as ye have beaten the poor with the fist, and taken choice gifts from him: ye have built houses, but ye shall not dwell in them: ye have planted pleasant vineyards, but ye shall not drink wine of them. For I know your manifold transgressions, in trampling justice beneath your foot, and taking a bribe, and turning aside the poor in the gate from their right. Therefore, the prudent shall keep

silence in that time, for it is an evil time."
Amos 5:11-13

Learn, beloved, the wickedness of the men of that time, how they spoil houses and fields, and take even justice from the just; for when these things come to pass, ye may know that it is the end. For this reason, art thou instructed in the wisdom of the prophet, and the revelation that is to be in those days. And all the prophets, as we have already said, have clearly signified the things that are to come to pass in the last times, just as they also have declared things of old.

6 The Church is Left Desolate, Continued

But not to expend our argument entirely in going over the words of all the prophets, after citing one other, let us revert to the matter in hand. What is it, then, that Micah says in his prophecy?

> "Thus saith the Lord concerning the prophets that make My people err, that bite with their teeth, and cry to him, Peace; and if it was not put into their mouth, they prepared war against him. Therefore, night shall be unto you, that ye shall not have a vision; and it shall be dark unto you, that ye shall not divine; and the sun shall not go down over the prophets, and the day shall be dark over them. And the seers shall be ashamed, and the diviners confounded." *Micah 3:5-7*

The End Times by the Ancient Church Fathers

These things we have recounted beforehand, in order that ye may know the pain that is to be in the last times, and the perturbation, and the manner of life on the part of all men toward each other, and their envy, and hate, and strife, and the negligence of the shepherds toward the sheep, and the unruly disposition of the people toward the priests.

7 End-Time Church Described

Wherefore all shall walk after their own will. And the children will lay hands on their parents. The wife will give up her own husband to death, and the husband will bring his own wife to judgment like a criminal. Masters will lord it over their servants savagely, and servants will assume an unruly demeanour toward their masters. None will reverence the grey hairs of the elderly, and none will have pity upon the comeliness of the youthful. The temples of God will be like houses, and there will be overturnings of the churches everywhere. The Scriptures will be despised, and everywhere they will sing the songs of the adversary. Fornications, adulteries, and perjuries will fill the land; sorceries, incantations, and divinations will follow after these with all force and zeal. And, on the whole, from among those who profess to be Christians, will rise up then false prophets, false apostles, impostors, mischief-makers, evil-doers, liars against each other, adulterers, fornicators, robbers, grasping, perjured, mendacious, hating each other. The shepherds will be like wolves; the priests will embrace falsehood; the monks will lust after the things of the world; the rich will assume hardness of heart; the rulers will not help the poor; the powerful will cast off all pity; the judges will remove justice from the just, and, blinded with bribes, they will call in unrighteousness.

8 The Signs

And what am I to say with respect to men, when the very elements themselves will disown their order? There will be earthquakes in every city, and plagues in every country; and monstrous thunderings and frightful lightnings will burn up both houses and fields. Storms of winds will disturb both sea and land excessively; and there will be unfruitfulness on the earth, and a roaring in the sea, and an intolerable agitation on account of souls and the destruction of men. There will be signs in the sun, and signs in the moon, deflections in the stars, distresses of nations, intemperateness in the atmosphere, discharges of hail upon the face of the earth, winters of excessive severity, different frosts, inexorable scorching winds, unexpected thunderings, unlooked-for conflagrations; and in general, lamentation and mourning in the whole earth, without consolation. For,

> "because iniquity shall abound, the love of many shall wax cold." *Matthew 24:12*

By reason of the agitation and confusion of all these, the Lord of the universe cries in the Gospel, saying,

> "Take heed that ye be not deceived; for many shall come in My name, saying, I am Christ, and the time draweth near: go ye not therefore after

them. But when ye shall hear of wars and commotions, be not terrified: for these things must first come to pass; but the end is not yet by and by." *Luke 21:8-9*

Let us observe the word of the Savior, how He always admonished us with a view to our security:

"Take heed that ye be not deceived: for many shall come in My name, saying, I am Christ." *Luke 21:8*

9 False Christs

Now after He was taken up again to the Father, there arose some, saying, "I am Christ," like Simon Magus[mm] and the rest, whose names we have not time at present to mention. Wherefore also in the last day of the consummation, it must needs be that false Christs will arise again, saying, "I am Christ," and they will deceive many. And multitudes of men will run from the east even to the west, and from the north even to the sea, saying, "Where is Christ here? Where is Christ there?" But being possessed of a vain conceit, and failing to read the Scriptures carefully[nn], and not being of an upright mind, they will seek for a name which they shall be unable to

---

[mm] Simon Magus was known as the father of the Gnostics. Gnosticism will return in the last days. Compare this to *Third Corinthians*.

[nn] We need to carefully study the Scriptures, especially the prophecies.

find. For these things must first be; and thus the son of perdition – that is to say, the devil – must be seen.

10-11 Heresies in the Church

And the apostles, who speak of God, in establishing the truth of the advent of the Lord Jesus Christ, have each of them indicated the appearing of these abominable and ruin-working men, and have openly announced their lawless deeds. First of all, Peter, the rock of the faith, whom Christ our God called blessed, the teacher of the church, the first disciple, he who has the keys of the kingdom, has instructed us to this effect:

> "Know this first, children, that there shall come in the last days scoffers, walking after their own lusts. *2 Peter 3:3*

> "And there shall be false teachers among you, who privily shall bring in damnable heresies."
> *2 Peter 2:1*

After him, John the theologian, and the beloved of Christ, in harmony with him, cries,

> "The children of the devil are manifest" *1 John 3:10*

> "and even now are there many antichrists" *1 John 2:18*

> "but go not after them." *Luke 21:8*

The End Times by the Ancient Church Fathers

> "Believe not every spirit, because many false prophets are gone out into the world." *1 John 4:1*

And then Jude, the brother of James, speaks in like manner:

> "In the last times there shall be mockers, walking after their own ungodly lusts... There be they who, without fear, feed themselves." *Jude 18, 12*

You have observed the concord of the theologians and apostles, and the harmony of their doctrine.

11 Heresies in the Church, Continued

Finally, hear Paul as he speaks boldly, and mark how clearly he discovers these:

> "Beware of evil workers, beware of the concision." *Philippians 3:2*

> "Beware lest any man spoil you through philosophy and vain deceit." *Colossians 2:8*

> "See that ye walk circumspectly, because the days are evil." *Ephesians 5:15-16*

What man, then, shall have any excuse who hears these things in the church from prophets and apostles, and from the Lord Himself, and yet will give no heed to the care of his soul, and to the time of the consummation, and to that approaching hour when we shall have to stand at the judgment seat of Christ?

12 Nebuchadnezzar's Great Image
But having now done with this account of the consummation, we shall turn our exposition to those matters which fall to be stated by us next in order. I adduce, therefore, a witness altogether worthy of credit, – namely, the prophet Daniel, who interpreted the vision of Nebuchadnezzar's, and from the beginning of the kings down to their end indicated the right way to those who seek to walk therein – to wit, the manifestation of the truth. For what did the prophet say? He declared the matter clearly to Nebuchadnezzar in the following terms:

> "Thou. O king, sawest, and behold a great image standing before thee, whose head was of gold, its arms and shoulders of silver, its belly and thighs of brass, its legs of iron, its feet part of iron and part of clay. Thou sawest till that a stone was cut out without hand; and it smote the image upon its feet, which were part of iron and part of clay, and brake them to pieces. Then was the clay, and the iron, and the brass, and the silver, and the gold broken to pieces together, and became like the chaff of the summer threshing-floor; and the stone that smote the image became a great mountain, and filled the whole earth." *Daniel 2:31-35*

13 Daniel's Vision of Beasts

Wherefore, bringing the visions of Daniel into conjunction with these, we shall make one narrative of the two, and show how true and consistent were the things seen in vision by the prophet with those which Nebuchadnezzar saw beforehand. For the prophet speaks thus:

"I Daniel saw, and, behold, the four winds of the heaven strove upon the great sea. And four great beasts came up from the sea, diverse one from another. The first was like a lioness, and had eagle's wings: I beheld till the wings thereof were plucked, and it was lifted up from the earth, and made stand upon the feet as a man, and a man's heart was given it. And behold a second beast, like to a bear, and it raised up itself on one side, and it had three ribs in the mouth of it between the teeth of it: and they said thus unto it, Arise, devour much flesh. After this I beheld, and lo a third beast, like a leopard, which had upon the back of it four wings of a fowl: the beast had also four heads. After this I saw, and behold a fourth beast, dreadful and terrible, and strong exceedingly; its great iron teeth and its claws of brass devoured and brake in pieces, and it stamped the residue with the feet of it: and it was diverse exceedingly from all the beasts that were before it; and it had ten horns. I considered its horns, and, behold, there came up among them a little horn, and before it there were three of the first horns plucked up by the roots: and, behold, in this horn were eyes like the eyes of man, and a mouth speaking great things." *Daniel 7:2-8*

14 Daniel's Lioness

Now, since these things which are thus spoken mystically by the prophet seem to all to be hard to understand, we shall conceal none of them from those who are possessed of sound mind. By mentioning the first beast, namely the lioness that comes up out of the sea, Daniel means the kingdom of the Babylonians which was set up in the world; and that same is also the "golden head" of this image. And by speaking of its "wings like an eagle," he shows that King Nebuchadnezzar was elevated and exalted himself against God. Then he says that its "wings were plucked out," and means by this that his glory was subverted: for he was driven from his kingdom. And in stating that a "man's heart was given it, and it was made to stand upon the feet like a man," he means that he repented, and acknowledged that he was himself but a man, and gave the glory to God. Lo, I have thus unfolded the similitude of the first beast.

15 Daniel's Bear and Leopard

Then after the lioness, the prophet sees a second beast like a bear, which denoted the Persians; for after the Babylonians the Persians had the sovereignty. And in saying, "I saw three ribs in the mouth of it," he referred to three nations, the Persians, Medes, and Babylonians, which were also expressed by the silver that came after the gold in the image. Behold, we have explained the second beast, too. Then the third was the leopard, by which were meant the Greeks. For after the Persians, Alexander, king of the Macedonians, held the sovereignty, when he had destroyed Darius; and this is expressed by the brass in the image. And in speaking of "four wings of a fowl, and four heads in the beast," he showed most clearly how the kingdom of Alexander was divided into four parts. For it had four heads, – namely, the four kings that rose out of it. For on his death-bed Alexander divided his kingdom into four parts. Behold, we have discussed the third also.

16-17 Daniel's Roman Beast

Next he tells us of the "fourth beast, dreadful and terrible; its teeth were of iron, and its claws of brass." And what is meant by these but the kingdom of the Romans, which also is meant by the iron, by which it will crush all the seats of empire that were before it, and will lord it over the whole earth? After this, then, what is left for us to interpret of all that the prophet saw, but the "toes of the image, in which part was of iron and part of clay, mingled together in one?" For by the ten toes of the image he meant figuratively the ten kings who sprang out of it, as Daniel also interpreted the matter. For he says, "I considered the beast, namely the fourth; and behold ten horns after it, among which another horn arose like an offshoot; and it will pluck up by the root three of those before it." And by this offshoot horn none other is signified than the Antichrist that is to restore the kingdom of the Jews. And the three horns which are to be rooted out by it signify three kings, namely those of Egypt,

Libya, and Ethiopia, whom he will destroy in the array of war; and when he has vanquished them all, being a savage tyrant, he will raise tribulation and persecution against the saints, exalting himself against them.

17 You see how Daniel interpreted to Nebuchadnezzar the dominion of the kingdoms; you see how he explained the form of the image in all its parts; you have observed how he indicated prophetically the meaning of the coming up of the four beasts out of the sea. It remains that we open up to you the things done by the Antichrist in particular; and, as far as in our power, declare to you by means of the Scriptures and the prophets, his wandering over the whole earth, and his lawless advent.

18a The Tribe of Judah

As the Lord Jesus Christ made His sojourn with us in the flesh which He received from the holy, immaculate virgin, and took to Himself the tribe of Judah, and came forth from it, the Scripture declared His royal lineage in the word of Jacob, when in his benediction he addressed himself to his son in these terms:

> "Judah, thou art he whom thy brethren shall praise: thy hands shall be on the neck of thine enemies; thy father's children shall bow down before thee. Judah is a lion's whelp; from a sprout, my son, thou art gone up: he stooped down, he couched as a lion, and as a lion's whelp: who shall rouse him up? A ruler shall not depart from Judah, nor a leader from his thighs, until

what is in store for him shall come, and he is the expectation of the nations." *Genesis 49:8-10*

Mark these words of Jacob which were spoken to Judah, and are fulfilled in the Lord. To the same effect, moreover, does the patriarch express himself regarding Antichrist.

18b-19 The Tribe of Dan

Wherefore, as he prophesied with respect to Judah, so did he also with respect to his son Dan. For Judah was his fourth son; and Dan, again, was his seventh son. And what, then, did he say of him?

> "Let Dan be a serpent sitting by the way, that biteth the horse's heel?" *Genesis 49:17*

And what serpent was there but the deceiver from the beginning, he who is named in Genesis, he who deceived Eve, and bruised Adam in the heel?

19 The Tribe of Dan, Continued

But seeing now that we must make proof of what is alleged at greater length, we shall not shrink from the task. For it is certain that he is destined to spring from the tribe of Dan, and to range himself in opposition like a princely tyrant, a terrible judge and accuser, as the prophet testifies when he says,

> "Dan shall judge his people, as one tribe in Israel." *Genesis 49:16*

The End of the World - Hippolytus

But someone may say that this was meant of Samson, who sprang from the tribe of Dan, and judged his people for twenty years. That, however, was only partially made good in the case of Samson; but this shall be fulfilled completely in the case of Antichrist. For Jeremiah, too, speaks in this manner:

> "From Dan we shall hear the sound of the sharpness of his horses; at the sound of the neighing of his horses the whole land trembled." *Jeremiah 8:16*

And again, Moses says:
> "Dan is a lion's whelp, and he shall leap from Bashan." *Deuteronomy 33:22*

And that no one may fall into the mistake of thinking that this is spoken of the Savior, let him attend to this. "Dan," says he, "is a lion's whelp;" and by thus naming the tribe of Dan as the one whence the accuser is destined to spring, he made the matter in hand quite clear. For as Christ is born of the tribe of Judah, so Antichrist shall be born of the tribe of Dan.[oo] And as our Lord and Savior Jesus Christ, the Son of God, was spoken of in prophecy as a lion on account or His royalty and glory, in the same manner also has the Scripture prophetically described the accuser as a lion, on account of his tyranny and violence.

[oo] Just as Bethlehem is inside the tribe of Judah so the birthplace of the Antichrist will be inside the tribe of Dan (Bashan). Jesus started his ministry in Zebulun and Naphtali.

20 Symbols of Christ and the Antichrist

For in every respect that deceiver seeks to make himself appear like the Son of God. Christ is a lion, and Antichrist is a lion. Christ is King of things celestial and things terrestrial, and Antichrist will be king upon earth. The Savior was manifested as a lamb; and he, too, will appear as a lamb, while he is a wolf within. The Savior was circumcised, and he in like manner will appear in circumcision. The Savior sent the apostles unto all the nations, and he in like manner will send false apostles. Christ gathered together the dispersed sheep, and he in like manner will gather together the dispersed people of the Hebrews. Christ gave to those who believed on Him the honorable and life-giving cross, and he in like manner will give his own sign. Christ appeared in the form of man, and he in like manner will come forth in the form of man. Christ arose from among the Hebrews, and he will spring from among the Jews. Christ displayed His flesh like a temple, and raised it up on the third day; and he too will raise up again the temple of stone in Jerusalem. And these deceits fabricated by him will become quite intelligible to those who listen to us attentively, from what shall be set forth next in order.

21 Enoch, Elijah, and John

For through the Scriptures we are instructed about the two advents of our Christ and Savior. And the first after the flesh was in humiliation, because He was manifested in lowly estate. So then His second advent is declared to be in glory; for He comes from heaven with power, and angels, and the glory of His Father. His first advent had

The End of the World - Hippolytus

John the Baptist as its forerunner; and His second, in which He is to come in glory, will exhibit Enoch, and Elias, and John the Divine[pp]. Behold, too, the Lord's kindness to man; how even in the last times He shows His care for mortals, and pities them. For He will not leave us even then without prophets, but will send them to us for our instruction and assurance, and to make us give heed to the advent of the adversary, as He intimated also of old in this Daniel. For he says,

> "I shall make a covenant of one week, and in the midst of the week my sacrifice and libation will be removed." *Daniel 9:27*

For by "one week" he indicates the showing forth of the seven years which shall be in the last times. And the half of the week the two prophets, along with John, will take for the purpose of proclaiming to all the world the advent of Antichrist, that is to say, for a

> "thousand two hundred and sixty days clothed in sackcloth;" *Revelation 11:3*

and they will work signs and wonders with the object of making men ashamed and repentant, even by these means, on account of their surpassing lawlessness and impiety. And if any man will hurt them, fire will proceed out of their mouth, and devour their enemies. These have power to shut heaven, that it rain not in the days of the advent of

---

[pp] See the notes in the summery chapter

Antichrist, and to turn waters into blood, and to smite the earth with all plagues as often as they will." And when they have proclaimed all these things, they will fall on the sword, cut off by the accuser. And they will fulfill their testimony, as Daniel also says; for he foresaw that the beast that came up out of the abyss would make war with them, namely with Enoch, Elias, and John, and would overcome them, and kill them, because of their refusal to give glory to the accuser, that is, the little horn that sprang up. And he, being lifted up in heart, begins in the end to exalt himself and glorify himself as God, persecuting the saints and blaspheming Christ.

22 Antichrist's Supposed Virgin Birth

But as, in accordance with the train of our discussion, we have been constrained to come to the matter of the days of the dominion of the adversary, it is necessary to state in the first place what concerns his nativity and growth; and then we must turn our discourse, as we have said before, to the expounding of this matter, viz., that in all respects the accuser and son of lawlessness [2 Thess. 2:4-8] is to make himself like our Savior. Thus also the demonstration makes the matter clear to us. Since the Savior of the world, with the purpose of saving the race of men, was born of the immaculate and virgin Mary, and in the form of the flesh trod the enemy under foot, in the exercise of the power of His own proper divinity; in the same manner also will the accuser come forth from an impure woman upon the earth, but shall be born of a virgin spuriously. For our God sojourned with us in the flesh, after that very flesh of ours which He made for

Adam and all Adam's posterity, yet without sin. But the accuser, though he take up the flesh, will do it only in appearance; for how should we wear that flesh which he did not make himself, but against which he warreth daily? And it is my opinion, beloved, that he will assume this phenomenal kind of flesh as an instrument. For this reason, also is he to be born of a virgin, as if a spirit, and then to the rest he will be manifested as flesh. For as to a virgin bearing, this we have known only in the case of the all-holy virgin, who bore the Savior verily clothed in flesh. For Moses says,

> "Every male that openeth the womb shall be called holy unto the Lord."
> Luke 2;23; Exodus 34:19

This is by no means the case with him; but as the adversary will not open the womb, so neither will he take to himself real flesh, and be circumcised[qq] as Christ was circumcised. And even as Christ chose His apostles, so will he too assume a whole people of disciples like himself in wickedness.

23-25a Antichrist's Deception
Above all, moreover, he will love the nation of the Jews.[rr] And with all these he will work signs and terrible wonders, false wonders and not true, in order to deceive his impious equals. For if it were possible, he would

---

[qq] Christians, Jews, and Muslims are circumcised.
[rr] Covet their land?

seduce even the elect [Matthew 24:24] from the love of Christ. But in his first steps he will be gentle, loveable, quiet, pious, pacific, hating injustice, detesting gifts, not allowing idolatry; loving, says he, the Scriptures, reverencing priests, honoring his elders, repudiating fornication, detesting adultery, giving no heed to slanders, not admitting oaths, kind to strangers, kind to the poor, compassionate. And then he will work wonders, cleansing lepers, raising paralytics, expelling demons, proclaiming things remote just as things present, raising the dead, helping widows, defending orphans, loving all, reconciling in love men who contend, and saying to such,

> "Let not the sun go down upon your wrath;"
> *Ephesians 4:26*

and he will not acquire gold, nor love silver, nor seek riches.

24 Antichrist's Deception, Continued

And all this he will do corruptly and deceitfully, and with the purpose of deluding all to make him king. For when the peoples and tribes see so great virtues and so great powers in him, they will all with one mind meet together to make him king. And above all others shall the nation of the Hebrews be dear to the tyrant himself, while they say one to another,

> "Is there found indeed in our generation such a man, so good and just?"

That shall be the way with the race of the Jews pre-eminently, as I said before, who, thinking, as they do, that they shall behold the king himself in such power, will approach him to say,

> "We all confide in you, and acknowledge you to be just upon the whole earth; we all hope to be saved by you; and by your mouth we have received just and incorruptible judgment."

25 Antichrist's Deception, Continued

And at first, indeed, that deceitful and lawless one, with crafty deceitfulness, will refuse such glory; but the men persisting, and holding by him, will declare him king. And thereafter he will be lifted up in heart, and he who was formerly gentle will become violent, and he who pursued love will become pitiless, and the humble in heart will become haughty and inhuman, and the hater of unrighteousness will persecute the righteous.

25b The Antichrist Wars

Then, when he is elevated to his kingdom, he will marshal war; and in his wrath he will smite three mighty kings, – those, namely, of Egypt, Libya, and Ethiopia.[ss] And after that he will build the temple in Jerusalem[tt], and will restore it again speedily, and give it over to the Jews. And then he will be lifted up in heart against every man; yea, he will speak blasphemy also against God, thinking in his

---

[ss] Modern-day Sudan.
[tt] Temple will be built after the three nations are destroyed.

deceit that he shall be king upon the earth hereafter forever; not knowing, miserable wretch, that his kingdom is to be quickly brought to naught, and that he will quickly have to meet the fire which is prepared for him, along with all who trust him and serve him. For when Daniel said,

> "I shall make my covenant for one week,"
> Daniel 9:27

he indicated seven years; and the one half of the week is for the preaching of the prophets, and for the other half of the week – that is to say, for three years and a half – Antichrist will reign upon the earth.[uu] And after this his kingdom and his glory shall be taken away. Behold, ye who love God, what manner of tribulation there shall rise in those days, such as has not been from the foundation of the world, no, nor ever shall be, except in those days alone. Then the lawless one, being lifted up in heart, will gather together his demons in man's form[vv], and will abominate those who call him to the kingdom, and will pollute many souls.

26a The Demonic Host

For he will appoint princes over them from among the demons. And he will no longer seem to be pious, but altogether and in all things he will be harsh, severe, passionate, wrathful, terrible, inconstant, dread, morose,

---

[uu] Two witnesses are in the first half of the seven-year period.
[vv] Demons in physical form.

The End of the World - Hippolytus

hateful, abominable, savage, vengeful, iniquitous. And, bent on casting the whole race of men into the pit of perdition, he will multiply false signs. For when all the people greet him with their acclamations at his displays, he will shout with a strong voice, so that the place shall be shaken in which the multitudes stand by him:

> "Ye peoples, and tribes, and nations, acquaint yourselves with my mighty authority and power, and the strength of my kingdom. What prince is there so great as I am? What great God is there but I? Who will stand up against my authority?"

26b False Signs

Under the eye of the spectators he will remove mountains from their places, he will walk on the sea with dry feet, he will bring down fire from heaven, he will turn the day into darkness and the night into day, he will turn the sun about wheresoever he pleases; and, in short, in presence of those who behold him, he will show all the elements of earth and sea to be subject to him in the power of his specious manifestation. For if, while as yet he does not exhibit himself as the son of perdition, he raises and excites against us open war even to battles and slaughters, at that time when he shall come in his own proper person, and men shall see him as he is in reality, what machinations and deceits and delusions will he not bring into play, with the purpose of seducing all men, and leading them off from the way of truth, and from the gate of the kingdom?

27 The Judgment

Then, after all these things, the heavens will not give their dew, the clouds will not give their rain, the earth will refuse to yield its fruits, the sea shall be filled with stench, the rivers shall be dried up, the fish of the sea shall die, men shall perish of hunger and thirst; and father embracing son, and mother embracing daughter, will die together, and there will be none to bury them. But the whole earth will be filled with the stench arising from the dead bodies cast forth. And the sea, not receiving the floods of the rivers, will become like mire, and will be filled with an unlimited smell and stench. Then there will be a mighty pestilence upon the whole earth, and then, too, inconsolable lamentation, and measureless weeping, and unceasing mourning. Then men will deem those happy who are dead before them, and will say to them, "Open your sepulchers, and take us miserable beings in; open your receptacles for the reception of your wretched kinsmen and acquaintances. Happy are ye, in that ye have not seen our days. Happy are ye, in that ye have not had to witness this painful life of ours, nor this irremediable pestilence, nor these straits that possess our souls."

28 The Mark

Then that abominable one will send his commands throughout every government by the hand at once of demons and of visible men, who shall say,

> "A mighty king has arisen upon the earth; come ye all to worship him; come ye all to see the strength of his kingdom: for, behold, he will give

you corn; and he will bestow upon you wine, and great riches, and lofty honors. For the whole earth and sea obeys his command. Come ye all to him."

And by reason of the scarcity of food, all will go to him and worship him; and he will put his mark on their right hand and on their forehead, that no one may put the sign of the honorable cross upon his forehead with his right hand; but his hand is bound. And from that time he shall not have power to seal any one of his members, but he shall be attached to the deceiver, and shall serve him; and in him there is no repentance. But such an one is lost at once to God and to men, and the deceiver will give them scanty food by reason of his abominable seal. And his seal upon the forehead and upon the right hand is the number,

>"Six hundred threescore and six."
>*Revelation 13:18*

And I have an opinion as to this number, though I do not know the matter for certain; for many names have been found in this number when it is expressed in writing. Still we say that perhaps the inscription of this same seal will give us the word "*I deny*." For even in recent days, by means of his ministers – that is to say, the idolaters – that bitter adversary took up the word *deny*, when the lawless pressed upon the witnesses of Christ, with the adjuration, "Deny thy God, the crucified One."

The End Times by the Ancient Church Fathers

29-30 Antichrist and the Two Witnesses

Of such kind, in the time of that hater of all good, will be the seal, the tenor of which will be this:

> "I deny the Maker of heaven and earth, I deny the baptism, I deny my former service, and attach myself to you, and I believe in you."

For this is what the prophets Enoch and Elias will preach:

> "Believe not the enemy who is to come and be seen; for he is an adversary, a corrupter, and son of perdition, and deceives you; and for this reason he will kill you, and smite them with the sword. Behold the deceit of the enemy, know the deception of the beguiler, how he seeks to darken the mind of men utterly."

For he will show forth his demons brilliant like angels, and he will bring in hosts of the incorporeal without number. And in the presence of all he exhibits himself as taken up into heaven with trumpets and sounds, and the mighty shouting of those who hail him with indescribable hymns; the heir of darkness himself shining like light, and at one time soaring to the heavens, and at another descending to the earth with great glory, and again charging the demons, like angels, to execute his behests with much fear and trembling. Then will he send the cohorts of the demons among mountains and caves and dens of the earth, to track out those who have been concealed from his eyes, and to bring them forward to

The End of the World - Hippolytus

worship him. And those who yield to him he will seal with his seal; but those who refuse to submit to him he will consume with incomparable pains and bitterest torments and machinations, such as never have been, nor have reached the ear of man, nor have been seen by the eye of mortals.

30 Blessed shall they be who overcome the tyrant then. For they shall be set forth as more illustrious and loftier than the first witnesses; for the former witnesses overcame his minions only, but these overthrow and conquer the accuser himself, the son of perdition. With what eulogies and crowns, therefore, will they not be adorned by our King, Jesus Christ!

31 The Minions of the Beast

But let us revert to the matter in hand. When men have received the seal, then, and find neither food nor water, they will approach him with a voice of anguish, saying, "Give us to eat and drink, for we all faint with hunger and all manner of straits; and bid the heavens yield us water, and drive off from us the beasts that devour men." Then will that crafty one make answer, mocking them with absolute inhumanity, and saying, "The heavens refuse to give rain, the earth yields not again its fruits; whence then can I give you food?" Then, on hearing the words of this deceiver, these miserable men will perceive that this is the wicked accuser, and will mourn in anguish, and weep vehemently, and beat their face with their hands, and tear their hair, and lacerate their cheeks with their nails, while they say to each other: "Woe for the calamity! woe for the bitter contract! woe for the deceitful covenant! woe for the mighty mischance! How have we been beguiled by the deceiver! how have we been joined to him! how have we been caught in his toils! how have we been taken in his abominable net! how have we heard the Scriptures, and understood them not!" For truly those who are engrossed with the affairs of life, and with the lust of this world, will be easily brought over to the accuser then, and sealed by him.

32 The Believers

But many who are hearers of the divine Scriptures, and have them in their hand, and keep them in mind with understanding, will escape his imposture. For they will see clearly through his insidious appearance and his deceitful imposture, and will flee from his hands, and betake themselves to the mountains, and hide themselves in the caves of the earth[ww]; and they will seek after the Friend of Man with tears and a contrite heart; and He will deliver them out of his toils, and with His right hand He will save those from his snares who in a worthy and righteous manner make their supplication to Him.

33-34 The Famines

You see in what manner of fasting and prayer the saints will exercise themselves at that time. Observe, also, how hard the season and the times will be that are to come upon those in city and country alike. At that time, they will be brought from the east even unto the west; and they

---

[ww] Matthew 24:16

The End of the World - Hippolytus

will come up from the west even unto the east, and will weep greatly and wail vehemently. And when the day begins to dawn they will long for the night, in order that they may find rest from their labors; and when the night descends upon them, by reason of the continuous earthquakes and the tempests in the air, they will desire even to behold the light of the day, and will seek how they may hereafter meet a bitter death [Deuteronomy 28:66-67]. At that time the whole earth will bewail the life of anguish, and the sea and air in like manner will bewail it; and the sun, too, will wail; and the wild beasts, together with the fowls, will wail; mountains and hills, and the trees of the plain, will wail on account of the race of man, because all have turned aside from the holy God, and obeyed the deceiver, and received the mark of that abominable one, the enemy of God, instead of the quickening cross of the Savior.

34 The Famines, Continued

And the churches, too, will wail with a mighty lamentation, because neither "oblation nor incense" is attended to, nor a service acceptable to God; but the sanctuaries of the churches will become like a garden-watcher's hut [Isaiah 1:8], and the holy body and blood of Christ will not be shown in those days. The public service of God shall be extinguished, psalmody shall cease, the reading of the Scriptures shall not be heard; but for men there shall be darkness, and lamentation on lamentation, and woe on woe. At that time silver and gold shall be cast out in the streets, and none shall gather them; but all things shall be held an offence. For all shall be eager to escape and to hide themselves, and they shall not be able anywhere to find concealment from the woes of the adversary; but as they carry his mark about them, they shall be readily recognized and declared to be his. Without there shall be fear, and within trembling, both by night and by day. In the streets and in the houses there shall be the dead; in the streets and in the houses there shall be hunger and thirst; in the streets there shall be tumults, and in the houses lamentations. And beauty of countenance shall be withered, for their forms shall be like those of the dead; and the beauty of women shall fade, and the desire of all men shall vanish.

35 Time Shortened

Notwithstanding, not even then will the merciful and benignant God leave the race of men without all comfort; but He will shorten even those days and the period of three years and a half, and He will curtail those times on account of the remnant of those who hide themselves in the mountains and caves, that the number of all those saints fail not utterly. But these days shall run their course rapidly; and the kingdom of the deceiver and Antichrist shall be speedily removed. And then, in fine, in the glance of an eye shall the fashion of this world pass away, and the power of men shall be brought to naught, and all these visible things shall be destroyed.

36 Second Coming of the Messiah

As these things, therefore, of which we have spoken before are in the future, beloved, when the one week is divided into parts, and the abomination of desolation has

The End of the World - Hippolytus

arisen then, and the forerunners of the Lord have finished their proper course, and the whole world, in fine, comes to the consummation, what remains but the manifestation of our Lord and Savior Jesus Christ, the Son of God, from heaven, for whom we have hoped; who shall bring forth fire and all just judgment against those who have refused to believe in Him? For the Lord says,

> "For as the lightning cometh out of the east, and shineth even unto the west, so shall also the coming of the Son of man be; for wheresoever the carcass is, there will the eagles be gathered together." *Matthew 24:27-28*

For the sign of the cross shall arise from the east even unto the west, in brightness exceeding that of the sun, and shall announce the advent and manifestation of the Judge, to give to every one according to his works. For concerning the general resurrection and the kingdom of the saints, Daniel says:

> "And many of them that sleep in the dust of the earth shall awake, some to everlasting life, and some to shame and everlasting contempt."
> *Daniel 12:2*

And Isaiah says:

> "The dead shall rise, and those in the tombs shall awake, and those in the earth shall rejoice."
> *Isaiah 26:19*

The End Times by the Ancient Church Fathers

And our Lord says:

> "Many in that day shall hear the voice of the Son of God, and they that hear shall live." *John 5:25*

37 Rapture or White Throne Judgment?

For at that time the trumpet shall sound [1 Thess. 4:16], and awake those that sleep from the lowest parts of the earth, righteous and sinners alike.[xx] And every kindred, and tongue, and nation, and tribe shall be raised in the twinkling of an eye [1 Cor. 15:52]; and they shall stand upon the face of the earth, waiting for the coming of the righteous and terrible Judge, in fear and trembling unutterable. For the river of fire shall come forth in fury like an angry sea, and shall burn up mountains and hills, and shall make the sea vanish, and shall dissolve the atmosphere with its heat like wax [2 Pet. 3:12]. The stars of heaven shall fall, [Matt. 24:29] the sun shall be turned into darkness, and the moon into blood [Acts 2:20]. The heaven shall be rolled together like a scroll [Rev. 6:14]: the whole earth shall be burnt up by reason of the deeds done in it, which men did corruptly, in fornications, in adulteries, and in lies and uncleanness, and in idolatries, and in murders, and in battles. For there shall be the new heaven and the new earth [Rev. 21:1].

38-40 Judgment of the Wicked

Then shall the holy angels run on their commission to gather together all the nations, whom that terrible voice of

---

[xx] He doesn't see the two separate resurrections.

the trumpet shall awake out of sleep. And before the judgment-seat of Christ shall stand those who once were kings and rulers, chief priests and priests; and they shall give an account of their administration, and of the fold, whoever of them through their negligence have lost one sheep out of the flock. And then shall be brought forward soldiers who were not content with their provision, but oppressed widows and orphans and beggars. Then shall be arraigned the collectors of tribute, who despoil the poor man of more than is ordered, and who make real gold like adulterate, in order to tax and fine the needy, in fields and in houses and in the churches. Then shall rise up the lewd with shame, who have not kept their bed undefiled, but have been ensnared by all manner of fleshly beauty, and have gone in the way of their own lusts. Then shall rise up those who have not kept the love of the Lord, mute and gloomy, because they contemned the light commandment of the Savior, which says, "Thou shalt love thy neighbor as thyself." Then they, too, shall weep who have possessed the unjust balance, and unjust weights and measures, and dry measures, as they wait for the righteous Judge.

39 Judgment of the Wicked, Continued

Then the righteous shall shine forth like the sun, while the wicked shall be shown to be mute and gloomy. For both the righteous and the wicked shall be raised incorruptible: the righteous, to be honored eternally, and to taste immortal joys; and the wicked, to be punished in judgment eternally. Each ponders the question as to what answer he shall give to the righteous Judge for his deeds, whether good or bad. With all men, each one's actions shall prove him, whether he be good or evil. For the powers of the heavens shall be shaken [Matt. 24:29], and fear and trembling shall consume all things, both heaven and earth and things under the earth. And every tongue shall confess Him openly [Phil. 2:11], and shall confess Him who comes to judge righteous judgment, the mighty God and Maker of all things. Then with fear and astonishment shall come angels, thrones, powers, principalities, dominions [Col. 1:16], and the cherubim and seraphim with their many eyes and six wings, all crying aloud with a mighty voice, "Holy, holy, holy is the Lord of hosts, omnipotent; the heaven and the earth are full of Thy glory." [Isaiah 6:3] And the King of kings and Lord of lords, the Judge who accepts no man's person, and the Jurist who distributes justice to every man, shall be revealed upon His dread and lofty throne; and all the flesh of mortals shall see His face with great fear and trembling, both the righteous and the sinner.

40 Judgment of the Wicked, Continued

Then shall the son of perdition be brought forward, to wit, the accuser, with his demons and with his servants, by angels stern and inexorable. And they shall be given over to the fire that is never quenched, and to the worm that never sleeps, and to the outer darkness. For the people of the Hebrews shall see Him in human form, as He appeared to them when He came by the holy virgin in the flesh, and as they crucified Him. And He will show them the prints of the nails in His hands and feet, and His side pierced with the spear, and His head crowned with thorns, and His honorable cross. And once for all shall the people of the Hebrews see all these things, and they shall mourn and weep, as the prophet exclaims,

> "They shall look on Him whom they have pierced;" *Zechariah 12:10; John 19:37*

and there shall be none to help them or to pity them, because they repented not, neither turned aside from the wicked way. And these shall go away into everlasting punishment with the demons and the accuser.

41 Sheep and Goat Judgement

Then He shall gather together all nations, as the holy Gospel so strikingly declares. For what says Matthew the evangelist, or rather the Lord Himself, in the Gospel?

> "When the Son of man shall come in His glory, and all the holy angels with Him, then shall He sit upon the throne of His glory: and before Him shall be gathered all nations; and He shall separate them one from another, as a shepherd divideth his sheep from the goats: and He shall set the sheep on His right hand, but the goats on the left. Then shall the King say unto them on His right hand, Come, ye blessed of My Father, inherit the kingdom prepared for you from the foundation of the world." *Matthew 25:31-34*

Come, ye prophets, who were cast out for My name's sake. Come, ye patriarchs, who before My advent were obedient to Me, and longed for My kingdom. Come, ye apostles, who were My fellows in My sufferings in My incarnation, and suffered with Me in the Gospel. Come, ye martyrs, who confessed Me before despots, and endured many torments and pains. Come, ye hierarchs, who did Me sacred service blamelessly day and night, and made the oblation of My honorable body and blood daily.

Summary of *On The End of the World*
In this second treatise, Hippolytus gives the same outline of prophecy but adds some interesting points:

- The Antichrist destroys water supplies [4]
- The apostasy of the church through sorcery [7]
- The apostasy of the church through Gnosticism [9].
- The Antichrist destroys three nations then builds the temple [25b].
- The two witnesses are in the first three-and-a-half years [25b].
- The last three-and-a-half-years will be shortened [35].

The End of the World - Hippolytus

Possible Problems Drifting In:
The Rapture in Chapter 37 seems to be mixed in with the Great White Throne judgment. Hippolytus could just be showing the Scripture in the same order the Old Testament prophets did and not explaining them as much, because he and the other ancient church fathers clearly taught a pre-trib Rapture.

Chapter 21 is interesting because Hippolytus and the other fathers have mentioned multiple times there are two witnesses who are called Enoch and Elijah. In this one chapter the subject is addressed again, but the only difference is that there are three witnesses, not two. Enoch, Elijah, and the apostle John. Either this is a confused scribe who accidentally added John to the mix, or someone is trying to tell us that in the end times there will be three records of witness:

1. The Book of Revelation written by the apostle John (this is included in the canon of Scripture).

2. The Book of Enoch which does contain prophecy for our generation but was never supposed to be added to the canon. (We have provided a modern translation with commentary for our readers in *The Ancient Book of Enoch*.)

3. The Ancient Book of Elijah. Both the Jewish Talmud and Josephus state that Elijah founded the school of the prophets and wrote an epistle to educate people into being "sons of the

prophets." There are several fake works by this name, but to my knowledge the real text is lost to us. However, if this is an accurate prophecy about the end times, someone will find this epistle and translate it.

Hippolytus' End-Time Outline

1. The Church shall apostatize [3, 5-6]
2. Weather extremes [8]
3. False christs appear [9]
4. Antichrist born from the tribe of Dan [18b-19]
5. Antichrist born of the circumcision [20, 22]
6. Antichrist says he is of Jewish descent [20]
7. Antichrist says he is virgin-born [22]
8. Antichrist claims to love Israel more than any one nation [24]

Seven Years Begin
9. Two Witnesses preach for 1260 days [21, 25b, 29-30]
10. Antichrist restores the kingdom of Jews [16]
11. Antichrist destroys Egypt, Libya, and Sudan [16, 25b]
12. Antichrist builds the Jerusalem temple [20, 25b]

Middle of the Seven Years
13. Antichrist stops temple sacrifices [21]
14. Persecution begins [16]
15. Antichrist creates the mark of the beast

End of the Seven Years
16. Second Coming
17. Destruction of the Antichrist and his empire

Conclusion

Pulling together all that Irenaeus, Hippolytus, Ephrem, and the other ancient church fathers teach, we can paint the following picture.

The Millennium
Approximately two thousand years after Jesus' death on the cross the Second Coming will occur. This will be the Jewish year 6,000 AM. We could pinpoint the exact day of the Second Coming if the Jewish Calendar were accurate, but we know it is off somewhere between 150 and 220 years. Jesus Christ will physically return to earth and set up a kingdom that will last one thousand years.

These ancient church fathers were all living in the second century AD. They taught the following prophecies would occur in this order:

Ancient Rome
1. Jerusalem destroyed by Rome (AD 70)
2. Nation of Israel dissolved (AD 132)
3. Roman Empire divided (AD 395)
4. Christian Byzantine Empire forms (AD 395)
5. Western Roman Empire dissolved (AD 476)
6. Desert peoples become senseless (Rise of Islam)
7. Byzantine-Persian wars (AD 602-628)
8. Christian Byzantine Empire overtaken (AD 1453)

The Church Would Apostatize
9. False christs would come
10. Gnosticism would return
11. Incantations and sorcery become common
12. Immorality becomes common
13. Study of prophecy forsaken

Prior to the Tribulation
14. The nation of Israel would be reborn (AD 1948)
15. Pre-temple sacrifices begin (AD 2014)
16. Weather extremes form

The Birth of the Antichrist
17. Antichrist born in Dan (Golan Heights)
18. Antichrist born of the circumcision (Jewish, Christian, or Muslim)
19. Antichrist says he is of Jewish descent
20. Antichrist says he is virgin born
21. Antichrist claims to love Israel more than any other nation

Toward the Beginning of the Seven Years
22. Worthless ten nations arise
23. Rapture of the church
24. Antichrist craftily takes the kingdom

During the First Half of the Tribulation Period
25. Two Witnesses preach for 1260 days
26. Antichrist raises up a religious Jewish kingdom
27. Antichrist appeases the Jews by reinstituting circumcision

28. Antichrist wars – Ps. 83
29. People hide in the rocks from the wars
30. Ammon and Moab surrender to Antichrist first
31. Tyre and Beirut, the first to fall to Antichrist
32. Antichrist destroys Egypt, Libya, and Sudan.
33. Antichrist restores Roman Empire from four pieces
34. The Jerusalem temple quickly rebuilt
35. Ten nations destroy Mystery Babylon

At the Middle of the Tribulation
36. Antichrist slays the two witnesses
37. Temple sacrifices stopped
38. Abomination set up in temple (for 1290 days)
39. Mark of the beast implemented
40. Ten nations persecute believers

During the Second Half of the Tribulation
41. God's wrath poured out
42. Believers flee Israel into the wilderness

The Second Coming
43. Jesus Christ returns to earth
44. Destruction of Antichrist and his kingdom
45. Establishment of the Millennium
46. Building of the Millennial temple

Questions to Consider
- Greece was depicted as a four-headed leopard and actually divided into four kingdoms. Medio-Persia was depicted as two arms of silver. Rome is depicted

Appendix B

as two iron legs. Does that mean five of the ten nations will come from the area of the western Roman Empire and five from the eastern Roman Empire (Byzantium)?

- Which Roman empire should we view for the area of the ten nations? Rome or Byzantium?
- Is the Psalm 83 war a reoccurring war that ends with the Antichrist's kingdom?
- Since the ten nations do not hold together, does that mean it cannot be a caliphate?
- Will the Antichrist be born in the Syrian Golan and rule from Damascus? Cities in the Syrian area of the Golan as of 2016 are: Bariqa, Beerajam, Al Qahtaniah, Al Qunaitra, El Hmidaiah, Jubata Al Khashab, Hader, Khan Arnabeh, Rwihinah, and Al Rafeed.

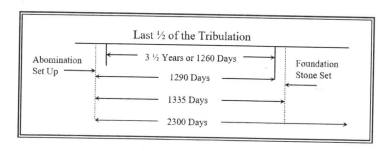

The chart above summarizes the ancient church fathers' outline of the last three-and-a-half years. If the 1260 days are the last three and a half years, then the 1290 days shows the abomination begins one month before the middle of the tribulation period and the 1335 days mark the time from the abomination of desolation to the setting the foundation stone of the millennial temple. The 2300

The End Times by the Ancient Church Fathers

days mark the time from the abomination to the dedication of the Millennial temple.

Appendix B

Index of Bible References

1 John 2:18 105
1 John 3:10 105
1 John 4:1 106
1 Thessalonians 4:13-17 93
1 Timothy 6:20-21 37
2 Peter 2:1 105
2 Peter 3:3 105
2 Thessalonians 2:1-11 89
2 Thessalonians 3:2 37
2 Timothy 2:1-2 37
Amos 5:11-13 101
Amos 6:18 25
Daniel 11:37 30
Daniel 11:41 77
Daniel 12:11-12 88
Daniel 12:2 .... 91, 129
Daniel 2:27 115
Daniel 2:31-35 .... 51, 107
Daniel 7:13-14 .... 53, 56, 69
Daniel 7:21,11 55
Daniel 7:2-8 .... 52, 109
Daniel 7:6 60
Daniel 7:8-9 72
Daniel 7:9-12 53
Daniel 9:27 .... 68, 120
Deuteronomy 32:34-35 82
Deuteronomy 33:22 .... 28, 45, 113
Ephesians 4:26 118
Ephesians 5:14 92
Ephesians 5:15-16 106
Exodus 34:19 117

The End Times by the Ancient Church Fathers

Ezekiel 28:2 78
Ezekiel 28:2-10 50
Ezekiel 28:9 79
Galatians 1:1 44
Genesis 49:16 .... 46, 112
Genesis 49:17 .... 46, 112
Genesis 49:8-10 112
Genesis 49:8-12 42
Hosea 13:15 100
Isaiah 1:21 43
Isaiah 1:7 99
Isaiah 1:7-8 58
Isaiah 10:12-17 48
Isaiah 11:1 43
Isaiah 11:14 77
Isaiah 14:13-15 79
Isaiah 14:4-21 49
Isaiah 18-1-2 83
Isaiah 23:4-5 78
Isaiah 26:10 89
Isaiah 26:19 .... 91, 129
Isaiah 26:20 91
Isaiah 33:17 69
Isaiah 47:1-15 62
Isaiah 53:2-5 69
Isaiah 66:24 93
Isaiah 8:6-7 82
Jeremiah 17:11 79
Jeremiah 4:11 81
Jeremiah 8:16 .... 47, 113
John 1:29 70
John 19:37 133
John 5:25 .... 91, 130
Jude 18-19 106
Luke 18:2-5 81
Luke 2;23 117

Appendix B

Luke 21:18 90
Luke 21:28 89
Luke 21:8 .... 104, 105
Luke 21:8-9 104
Malachi 4:2 87
Malachi 4:5-6 71
Matthew 13:43 92
Matthew 24:12 103
Matthew 24:15-22 87
Matthew 24:27-28 .... 90, 129
Matthew 24:31 90
Matthew 25:31-34 133
Matthew 25:34 92
Matthew 25:41 92
Matthew 5:18 98
Micah 3:5-7 101
Micah 5:5 82
Philippians 3:2 106
Psalm 110:1 86
Psalm 19:6 90
Psalm 3:5 43
Psalm 83:8 29
Revelation 11:3 .... 71, 86, 115
Revelation 11:4-6 72
Revelation 11:7 72
Revelation 12:1-6 85
Revelation 13:11-18 74
Revelation 13:18 .... 76, 123
Revelation 17:1-18 65
Revelation 17:9 58
Revelation 18:1-24 67
Revelation 20:6 92
Revelation 22:15 92
Romans 1:17 91
Titus 2:13 94
Zechariah 12:10 133

Other Books and DVDs by Ken Johnson, Th.D.

Ancient Post-Flood History
Historical Documents That Point to a Biblical Creation.
This book is a Christian timeline of ancient post-Flood history based on Bible chronology, the early church fathers, and ancient Jewish and secular history. This can be used as a companion guide in the study of Creation Science. Some questions answered: Who were the Pharaohs in the times of Joseph and Moses? When did the famine of Joseph occur? What Egyptian documents mention these? When did the Exodus take place? When did the Kings of Egypt start being called "Pharaoh" and why? Who was the first king of a united Italy? Who was Zeus and where is he buried? Where did Shem and Ham rule and where are they buried? How large was Nimrod's invasion force that set up the Babylonian Empire, and when did this invasion occur? What is Nimrod's name in Persian documents? How can we use this information to witness to unbelievers?

Ancient Seder Olam
A Christian Translation of the 2000-year-old Scroll
This 2000-year-old scroll reveals the chronology from Creation through Cyrus' decree that freed the Jews in 536 BC. The Ancient Seder Olam uses biblical prophecy to prove its calculations of the timeline. We have used this technique to continue the timeline all the way to the reestablishment of the nation of Israel in AD 1948. Using the Bible and rabbinical tradition, this book shows that the ancient Jews awaited King Messiah to fulfill the prophecy spoken of in Daniel, Chapter 9. The Seder answers many questions about the chronology of the books of Kings and

Chronicles. It talks about the coming of Elijah, King Messiah's reign, and the battle of Gog and Magog.

Ancient Prophecies Revealed
500 Prophecies Listed In Order Of When They Were Fulfilled

This book details over 500 biblical prophecies in the order they were fulfilled; these include pre-flood times though the First Coming of Jesus and into the Middle Ages. The heart of this book is the 53 prophecies fulfilled between 1948 and 2008. The last 11 prophecies between 2008 and the Tribulation are also given. All these are documented and interpreted from the Ancient Church Fathers. The Ancient Church Fathers, including disciples of the twelve apostles, were firmly premillennial, pretribulational, and very pro-Israel.

Ancient Book of Jasher
Referenced in Joshua 10:13; 2 Samuel 1:18; 2 Timothy 3:8

There are thirteen ancient history books mentioned and recommended by the Bible. The Ancient Book of Jasher is the only one of the thirteen that still exists. It is referenced in Joshua 10:13; 2 Samuel 1:18; and 2 Timothy 3:8. This volume contains the entire ninety-one chapters plus a detailed analysis of the supposed discrepancies, cross-referenced historical accounts, and detailed charts for ease of use. As with any history book, there are typographical errors in the text but with three consecutive timelines running though the histories, it is very easy to arrive at the exact dates of recorded events. It is not surprising that this ancient document confirms the Scripture and the chronology given in the Hebrew version of the Old Testament, once and for all settling the chronology differences between the Hebrew Old Testament and the Greek Septuagint.

Third Corinthians
Ancient Gnostics and the End of the World
This little known, 2000-year-old Greek manuscript was used in the first two centuries to combat Gnostic cults. Whether or not it is an authentic copy of the original epistle written by the apostle Paul, it gives an incredible look into the cults that will arise in the Last Days. It contains a prophecy that the same heresies that pervaded the first century church would return before the Second Coming of the Messiah.

Ancient Paganism
The Sorcery of the Fallen Angels
Ancient Paganism explores the false religion of the ancient pre-Flood world and its spread into the Gentile nations after Noah's Flood. Quotes from the ancient church fathers, rabbis, and the Talmud detail the activities and beliefs of both Canaanite and New Testament era sorcery. This book explores how, according to biblical prophecy, this same sorcery will return before the Second Coming of Jesus Christ to earth. These religious beliefs and practices will invade the end time church and become the basis for the religion of the Antichrist. Wicca, Druidism, Halloween, Yule, meditation, and occultic tools are discussed at length.

The Rapture
The Pretribulational Rapture of the Church Viewed From the Bible and the Ancient Church
This book presents the doctrine of the pretribulational Rapture of the church. Many prophecies are explored with Biblical passages and terms explained. Evidence is presented that proves the first century church believed the End Times would begin with the return of Israel to her ancient homeland, followed by the Tribulation and the Second Coming. More than fifty prophecies have been fulfilled since Israel became a state. Evidence is also given that several ancient rabbis and at least four ancient church fathers taught a pretribulational Rapture. This book also

gives many of the answers to the arguments midtribulationists and posttribulationists use. It is our hope this book will be an indispensable guide for debating the doctrine of the Rapture.

Ancient Epistle of Barnabas
His Life and Teaching
The Epistle of Barnabas is often quoted by the ancient church fathers. Although not considered inspired Scripture, it was used to combat legalism in the first two centuries AD. Besides explaining why the Laws of Moses are not binding on Christians, the Epistle explains how many of the Old Testament rituals teach typological prophecy. Subjects explored are: Yom Kippur, the Red Heifer ritual, animal sacrifices, circumcision, the Sabbath, Daniel's visions and the end-time ten nation empire, and the temple. The underlying theme is the Three-Fold Witness. Barnabas teaches that mature Christians must be able to lead people to the Lord, testify to others about Bible prophecy fulfilled in their lifetimes, and teach creation history and creation science to guard the faith against the false doctrine of evolution. This is one more ancient church document that proves the first century church was premillennial and constantly looking for the Rapture and other prophecies to be fulfilled.

The Ancient Church Fathers
What the Disciples of the Apostles Taught
This book reveals who the disciples of the twelve apostles were and what they taught, from their own writings. It documents the same doctrine was faithfully transmitted to their descendants in the first few centuries and where, when, and by whom, the doctrines began to change. The ancient church fathers make it very easy to know for sure what the complete teachings of Jesus and the twelve apostles were. You will learn, from their own writings, what the first century disciples taught about the various doctrines that

divide our church today. You will learn what was discussed at the seven general councils and why. You will learn who were the cults and cult leaders that began to change doctrine and spread their heresy and how that became to be the standard teaching in the medieval church. A partial list of doctrines discussed in this book are:

Abortion	Mary's virginity
Animal sacrifices	Mary's assumption
Antichrist	Meditation
Arminianism	The Nicolaitans
Bible or tradition	Paganism
Calvinism	Predestination
Circumcision	Premillennialism
Deity of Jesus Christ	Purgatory
Demons	Psychology
Euthanasia	Reincarnation
Evolution	Replacement theology
False gospels	Roman Catholicism
False prophets	The Sabbath
Foreknowledge	Salvation
Free will	Schism of Nepos
Gnostic cults	Sin / Salvation
Homosexuality	The soul
Idolatry	Spiritual gifts
Islam	Transubstantiation
Israel's return	Yoga
Jewish food laws	Women in ministry

Ancient Book of Daniel

The ancient Hebrew prophet Daniel lived in the fifth century BC and accurately predicted the history of the nation of Israel from 536 BC to AD 1948. He also predicted the date of the death of the Messiah to occur in AD 32, the date of the rebirth of the nation of Israel to occur in AD 1948, and the Israeli capture of the Temple Mount to take place in AD 1967! Commentary from the ancient rabbis and the first century church reveals how the messianic rabbis and the disciples of the apostles interpreted his prophecies. Daniel also indicated where the Antichrist would come from, where he would place his international headquarters, and identified the three rebel nations that will attack him during the first three-and-a-half years of the Tribulation.

Ancient Epistles of John and Jude
This book provides commentary for the epistles of John and Jude from the ancient church fathers. It gives the history of the struggles of the first century church. You will learn which cults John and Jude were writing about and be able to clearly identify each heresy. You will also learn what meditation and sorcery truly are. At the end of each chapter is a chart contrasting the teaching of the church and that of the Gnostics. Included are master charts of the doctrine of Christ, the commandments of Christ, and the teaching of the apostles.

Learn the major doctrines that all Christians must believe: Jesus is the only Christ, Jesus is the only Savior, Jesus is the only begotten Son of God, Jesus is sinless, Jesus physically resurrected, Jesus will physically return to earth, God is not evil, The Rapture, Creationism, Eternal life only by Jesus, The sin nature, Prophecy proves inspiration, Idolatry is evil

Ancient Messianic Festivals,
And The Prophecies They Reveal
The messianic festivals are the biblical rituals God commanded the ancient Israelites to observe. These ancient rites give great detail about the First Coming of the Messiah including the date on which He would arrive, the manner of His death, and the birth of His church. You will also learn of the many disasters that befell the Jews through the centuries on the ninth of Av. The rituals speak of a Natzal, or rapture of believers, and a terrible time called the Yamin Noraim. They give a rather complete outline of this seven-year

tribulation period, including the rise of a false messiah. They also tell of a time when the earth will be at peace in the Messianic Kingdom. In addition to the seven messianic festivals, you will learn the prophetic outline of other ceremonies like Hanukkah, the new moon ceremony, the wedding ceremony, the ashes of the red heifer, and the ancient origins of Halloween. You will also learn of other prophetical types and shadows mentioned in the Bible.

Ancient Word of God
Is there a verse missing from your Bible? Would you like to know why it was removed? This book covers the history of the transmission of the Bible text through the centuries. It examines and proves, based on fulfilled Bible prophecy, which Greek texts faithfully preserve the ancient Word of God. You will learn about the first century cults that created their own warped Bibles and of the warnings that the ancient church gave in regard to the pure text. Over two hundred English Bibles are compared. Is the KJV more accurate, maybe the NIV, or perhaps the NASB or ESV?

Cults and the Trinity
This book compares Christianity with the false religions of the world today based on the accuracy of fulfilled Bible prophecy. No other religion has used prophecy fulfilled in the reader's lifetime to prove its authority, except the Bible. With more than fifty prophecies fulfilled since AD 1948, and Jesus' teaching that He is the only way to salvation, we can conclude we must be a Christian to gain eternal life. Jesus declares you must follow His teachings in order to obtain eternal life. Among these teachings is the fact that Jesus is God incarnate, the second person of the Trinity. Numerous church fathers' quotes dating back to the first century AD show this fact as well, and the ancient church defined a cult as a group claiming to be Christian but denying the Trinity. Listing over one hundred cults and numerous subgroups, this book shows that virtually all of

them are nontrinitarians. A detailed, yet simple, study on the Trinity will enable you to witness to all the cults using only this one doctrine.

Ancient Book of Enoch
The Holy Spirit inspired Jude to quote Enoch for a reason. The Ancient Book of Enoch opens by addressing those in the Tribulation period. It contains numerous prophecies about the flood and fire judgments, and the two comings of the Messiah. It teaches that the Messiah is the Son of God and that He will shed His blood to redeem us and even predicts the generation that this would occur!

The book of Enoch prophesies a window of time in which the Second Coming would occur and prophesies that there will be twenty-three Israeli Prime Ministers ruling in fifty-eight terms from AD 1948 to the beginning of the Tribulation period, and much more. Even though it prophecies that the Bible would be created and says we will be judged by our obedience to the Bible, it also makes it clear that this book is not to be added to the Canon of Scripture.

The Ancient Book of Enoch recounts the history of the angels who fell in the days of Jared, Enoch's father. It testifies to their marriages with human women and their genetic experiments. This commentary includes a previously unknown chapter from the Dead Sea Scrolls that actually explains how they did their genetic tampering.

Ancient Epistles of Timothy and Titus
This book provides commentary for the epistles of Timothy and Titus from the ancient church fathers. It describes the history of the struggles of the first century church. It reveals which heretics and cults Paul was writing about. It details the history of those heretics and their errors. Learn which Gnostic cults Alexander, Demas, Hymenaeus, Philetus,

Phygellus, and Hermogenes were involved in, what heresies they taught, and exactly why Paul excommunicated them. At the end of each chapter is a chart contrasting the teaching of the church and that of the Gnostics. Included are master charts of sound doctrine, the commandments of Christ, and the teaching of the apostles.

Fallen Angels
Using only the Bible, Dead Sea Scrolls, the writings of the ancient rabbis, and the writings of the ancient church fathers, this book puts together the history of the creation of angelic beings, the fall of Lucifer and his angels, the fall of Azazel, and the fall of Samyaza and his angels. Learn the history of the Nephilim (giants) both pre-flood and post-flood. Find details of many angels, demons, and nephilim in the dictionary at the back of the book. Even find out the exact location on earth of the fallen angel Azazel.

Ancient Book of Jubilees
Almost lost over the centuries, the Book of Jubilees was retrieved from the Ethiopic language and was recently found among the Dead Sea Scrolls. The Book of Jubilees is also called the Little Genesis, Book of Divisions, and the Apocalypse of Moses. It repeats the events of Genesis and Exodus from Creation to the Exodus of the Children of Israel from Egypt. It recounts the events in sets of jubilees (sets of 49 years) and gives additional details such as the fall of the angels, and the creation and destruction of the Nephilim. It also mentions the three classes of pre-flood Nephilim. It details the fact that one-tenth of their disembodied spirits would remain on earth as demons to tempt people and nine-tenths would be chained until the Tribulation Period. Learn what secrets this Dead Sea Scroll holds. Compare the mysterious Qumran calendar with that of the Bible to learn more about biblical prophecies. The commentary is written from a fundamentalist Christian perspective.

The Gnostic Origins of Calvinism

This book traces the history of Calvinistic thought and its infiltration into the church through the centuries. We start with the Valentinian Gnostics of the first and second centuries and catalog the reaction of the ancient church fathers. We then jump to the Gnostic Manicheans with Augustine and Pelagius in the fifth century AD. Finally, we arrive at Calvin and Knox, who formed modern Calvinism with its acceptance into Protestant thought in the fifteenth century, and the reaction to Calvinism by Jacob Arminius. After looking at the history of Calvinism, we will examine the doctrine of Calvinism and compare it to the doctrines of the Bible and the first century church. Quotes from the church fathers can be read in their entirety in the ten-volume set of *Ante-Nicene Fathers*, and summarized in *Ancient Church Fathers*.

The Gnostic Origins of Roman Catholicism

The ancient church fathers documented their struggle with the rebellion of the bishops of Rome. They recorded the heresies that crept into the Roman Catholic Church and their subsequent rebuke of those Roman bishops, or popes. The first section will give a detailed history of Rome from AD 50 to modern times. The second section will deal with some ancient prophecies about the rise and fall of papal Rome. The third section deals directly with some of the major divisive issues created by the Roman Catholic Church, such as: papal infallibility, idolatry, sorcery, transubstantiation, celibacy, purgatory, etc. The true origin of these doctrinal heresies are the Gnostic cults of the first and second century. Quotes from the church fathers can be read in their entirety in the ten volume set of *Ante-Nicene Fathers*, and summarized in *Ancient Church Fathers*.

Demonic Gospels

Learn how we got the books of the Bible. There were prophets who proved they were from God by performing miracles and making localized predictions with one hundred percent accuracy. Their long-range predictions were then recorded in the sixty-six books of the Bible. We can know this for a fact because over fifty of those long-range prophecies have come to pass since the nation of Israel was reborn in AD 1948. The ancient church fathers teach the gnostic gospels were demonically inspired. They contain no prophecy and their teachings contradict the teachings of the prophetically proven Word of God. In some cases the church fathers record which cults wrote which gnostic books and why they are to be considered heresy. The demonic gnostic gospels teach reincarnation, that there are multiple gods, and that humans are divine. They teach that the use of sorcery is imperative for salvation. The Bible clearly teaches that there is only one God. We do not have a spark of God in us, nor are we evolving into gods. It also teaches that the use of sorcery is a sin that will damn people to an eternal hell, and that everyone will die only once, physically resurrect, and be judged. The gnostic gospels are summarized in their own chapters showing why these are truly demonic gospels!

The Pre-Flood Origins of Astrology
What is modern astrology and why are so many people fascinated with it? Where did it come from and is there any truth to it? Find out what the sun, moon, and planets are for, according to the Bible, then see how the ancient pre-flood world perverted that knowledge to form a type of proto-astrology. Learn how and when the horoscope was invented and how it is used in the occult world. Learn what wise men who followed the star of Bethlehem knew from the Bible and the wise men's own account of what they experienced. From these records, the Dead Sea Scrolls, and the books of Enoch, Jasher, and Josephus, we learn the history of astrology and why Christians should not be involved with it. Numerous scientific studies are also examined in this work.

The Prophecy Series DVDs

DVD 1 – The Prophetic Timeline
In This DVD, you will learn the biblical outline of prophecy from the book of Daniel. The prophet Daniel accurately predicted the exact day of the Messiah's first coming and the exact dates of the return of the State of Israel on May 14, 1948 and the capture of the Temple Mount on June 7, 1967! Many more fulfilled prophecies are given with their respective dates. You will also learn about the yet-to-be-fulfilled prophecies including the Great Tribulation.

DVD 2 – The Church Age
In this DVD, you will learn the three prophetical ages of Israel that exist during the seven prophetical ages of the Church. You will learn about the Prophecies that were fulfilled in the first century and in the Middle Ages, what the ancient church fathers taught about premillennialism, and the prophecies about the church age itself from the Old Testament. Finally, we will learn how the Bible and ancient church fathers describe the prophesied apostasy in its finished state at the end of days.

For more information, visit us at:

Biblefacts.org

Bibliography

Eerdmans Publishing, *Ante-Nicene Fathers*, Eerdmans Publishing, 1886
David Bercot, *A Dictionary of Early Christian Beliefs*, Hendrickson Publishers, 1999
Cruse, C. F., *Eusebius' Ecclesiastical History*, Hendrickson Publishers, 1998
Ken Johnson, *Ancient Church Fathers*, Createspace, 2010
Ken Johnson, *Third Corinthains*, Createspace, 2008
Ken Johnson, *Gnostic Origins of Roman Catholicism*, Createspace, 2013

Made in the USA
Middletown, DE
24 April 2018